T0370495

Something

poetry & pictures by

KAYLA BATTLE

AuthorHouse™
1663 Liberty Drive
Bloomington, IN 47403
www.authorhouse.com
Phone: 1 (800) 839-8640

Because of the dynamic nature of the Internet, any web addresses or links contained in this book may have changed
since publication and may no longer be valid. The views expressed in this work are solely those of the author and do not
necessarily reflect the views of the publisher, and the publisher hereby disclaims any responsibility for them.

Any people depicted in stock imagery provided by Getty Images are models,
and such images are being used for illustrative purposes only.
Certain stock imagery © Getty Images.

This book is printed on acid-free paper.

ISBN: 978-1-5462-2199-9 (sc)
ISBN: 978-1-5462-2200-2 (e)

Library of Congress Control Number: 2019910632

Print information available on the last page.

Published by AuthorHouse 08/15/2019

author**HOUSE**®

To anyone who's ever confiscated my hopes and dreams
and gave it back.
This is the result of that.

Not a lot of pages in this book are
extraordinary or noteworthy,
but they were instances that helped me to keep going.

Not a lot of moments in life are going to be
phenomenal or spectacular,
but you must always keep going.

IF YOU DON'T TRY, YOU FAIL

The sunsets at the intersection.

Cars drive by, driving to and from.

I'm sitting with my cats,

wondering what am I trying to latch onto?

Preferably someone but possibly no one.

I'll wait until she says "hey" again.

Wasting away until that day again.

Our first conversation, she mentioned her favorite book

I can't remember the title of.

I'll have to keep writing, maybe I'll catch her attention,

maybe then, I can write about love.

There'll be so much to edit. So much to work with,

but how can I forget it's everything I've ever wanted?

How can I be such a tarnishing disappointment?

Although if I'm being realistic,

just from what I know, from my own experience,

new beginnings means a new disaster.

May as well just set myself on fire.

I'm just lonely and I don't know what to do

except be an idiot and wish I was enough for you.

When will I come across someone that I make sense to?

When will I win over someone's point of view?

I just want to escape to evade the overbearing emptiness,

the overwhelming weight, I'm too much to take in.

Is anybody listening to what I have to say

or is everybody just expecting me to lead the way?

It's stressful when no one takes me seriously

yet I'm the only leader apparently.

TONIGHT WON'T BE MY LAST

Here I am, scratching my head
wondering what will lie ahead
and I know I won't know,
if tonight I let go.

I hate the way things are going
but if I dare make that choice – I'm knowing
if I let go tonight,
I might not see that heavenly light.

I get told to just move on,
but it's not easy with you now gone.
I think you made a mistake.
Now everything feels to be at stake.

I don't want to miss out
on what my future could be about.
I may regret the past
but tonight won't be my last.

SILENTLY SCREAMING
(FALLING HEADFIRST FROM HEAVEN)

I can't survive here all alone.
I'm supposed to call it a home
but my home is with you,
and I'm so far away from that.
I need you to hold me now
but who knows where the hell you are.
What is love exactly?
Is it supposed to make you happy?
Rejected hand after hand but you're the one.
Can you hear me scream your name?

My soul is screaming in pain.
This emptiness drives me insane.
Every second I shed a tear
because you're not here,
and you can't hear me
but somehow, I feel you hold me up.
Is it really you? It cannot be
because you're nowhere near I can see
but I feel the wholeness inside
so I know it's you.

No doubt in my mind you knew
I was silently screaming.
So I will hold on for you
and just keep dreaming.

ANSWERS OR ANGER

I'll never give up every time I get in a fight with you.
Why can't my questions have answers to follow through?
You think you're right but please speak for yourself.
You can't dictate the lives of anyone else.

You can say what's wrong and what's right
but you can't tell me how to live my life.
Scream and yell to release your anger on me
and pretend I'm obligated to be happy.

I don't care how your day was.
You just don't get when I've had enough.
Back off, I don't care.
Let me breathe my own air.

Despite how many times I get put on trial
for not lying and following along,
I won't stay here and pretend to smile.
I have to go back to where I belong.

EMPTY HANDS

Tell me not to leave you,
even though I can't ever feel you care.
Tell me to run to you,
but it's too dark and I can't see you there.

Tell me what to do,
and it's already done for you.
I'll be what you want me to be,
you won't need to wait and see.

Failed another test.
Feeling so depressed.
Everything's a mess.
Am I just obsessed?

I can't live without you.
I can't stand all alone.
I can't wait until we say 'I do.'
You mean more than anyone I've known.

Always stay here.
Come running without any fears.
Shed no more tears.
Live through all our happy years.

Take my heart and I'll take yours
and we'll run to a place that no one knows.
Let's just run into the depths of forever.
Even in death, our souls can bond together.

I'll protect you from the light when it tries to burn your eyes.
I'll save you from the sanity when it crosses your mind.
I'd give up anything right now to hold you in my arms
and anything for you to feel my love in your heart.

If there's any part of me that you can't stand,
don't worry, I'll understand.
I'll do all I can to make things right again,
just don't leave me with empty hands.

LIKE BEFORE

They're all busy, no one has time for you now.
No one has time for your ongoing breakdowns.
Hold yourself together,
things get a lot better.

People suck but that's your luck.
Take in the pain like you want more.
Why care when life isn't fair?
Just don't let things go like before.

Your purpose here might be gone.
Unless you're ready, how do you move on?
New opportunities are out there,
you just need to find out where.

Everything happens for a reason.
Every word written has a meaning.
Someone might care if you're not breathing.
The world's not ready for your leaving.

IT'S NOT THAT BAD

The days will go by.
The bad things will disappear.
Everything will be fine.
I should stay here.
It's not hopeless yet.
It's not that bad.
The worst it can get
is when I lose what I have.

Things are overwhelming I'll admit, I won't deny
but someday things will be better.
I've been through much worse shit, wanting to die
but my hopes keep me together.

Keep the smile on your face.
Everything will be alright.
Please remind me it's okay.
I feel so alone tonight.
I feel insecure.
Lost in a fucked-up world.
Everything's a blur.
Unhappy, that's for sure.

DISEASE

Right now, as I write this down,
I feel the same grip I can never get rid of.
I've tried so hard but it's impossible.
I've tried almost everything
but this crush is unstoppable.
Get this disease out of me.

It hurts so much to be without you
besides feeling mentally ill, too.
Your picture's in front of me
in black and white.
Is that the way you see life?
The disease is in you too.

Born like this, this is who we are.
No one can change us, not even ourselves.
We're monsters of the earth.
Our fate is to take the abuse of the world,
alone, without each other's help.
The disease is spreading rapidly.

I still believe there must be a way
for all of us to understand
but it seems two eyes, a beating heart, a functional brain
isn't enough to know we must act humane
Maybe it's silly to have a dream
as if this disease can be beat.

OUR GENERATION

"The end is near."
I don't know how we've come so far
living in fear.
What's wrong with my belief?
The freedom of religion is such a relief.
Let's separate church and state.
We don't want to live with these inhibitions.
Eyes on the president.
His actions represent our lives,
and what happens to our descendants.

We can't go on living this way.
Look in our hearts, desperate for a change.
Just check it for a second,
shouldn't something so outdated be questioned?
It doesn't work with this generation.
I don't want your tradition and dreams,
and I don't want your religions.
I don't want what you think is best for me
or your differing opinions.
Our generation is the future of this nation.

THE TRUTH

The secret you want me to keep
is written with a stencil
and now it's erased from this page,
all the plans have been cancelled.

I know the truth.
I know all the words you wouldn't tell me.
I still love you
and all the thoughts that could all be...
Put together with the guide of a falling feather
from an innocent bird that's passed away.
The destructive disease that's such a tease,
there's just no hope for life today.

I know the truth.
I know all the words you wouldn't tell me.
I still love you
and all the thoughts that could all be...
The one to tell me
this is the way things are meant to be.
What happens is supposed to happen
so, tell the demons to stop laughing.

Your Secret Admirer

It's alright. Don't be shy.
Don't be scared.
If you need me, I'll be there.

I don't know exactly how this all began
but it has and I want to let you know,
don't be afraid to decide to stay.

I like you the way you are.
You don't have to change.
Let go of fear, it's okay.

I feel this getting stronger,
I don't know how much longer
I can let this build.
When I see you, I feel completely filled.

I don't know why,
it just is.
Don't tell me
I can change this.

Just please say there's a chance,
a chance for us,
a chance for just
this innocent love.

Do you even know it's me?
-Your secret admirer.

WAKE UP (IF YOU'RE STILL ALIVE)

Nothing seems real right now,
like everything's turned into a lie somehow.
It's like I'm not really here.
The truth is so unclear.

I open my window and let the cold air in.
I hope someday you'll wake up and call for me.
I suddenly realize it's emptiness trapped within.
I'm alone and my body is getting cold.

I know what it's like to have no one understand
because I've been through it too.
Always constantly reaching out your hand
but no one knows what you're going through.

All you've ever wanted was to hear someone say
"I'll die for you" and actually mean it.
How can you expect such words at this age?
Everyone deserves a chance to begin.

I open my window and let the cold air in.
I wish you would wake up and realize
even though you're hurting a lot deep within,
things will get better if you stay alive.

I'm going to make you happier somehow.
I'm going to take care of you.
I promise you right now,
you'll be glad you got through.

Never Good Enough

I've worked so hard
but still I've managed an F on my report card.
I don't know how I've come so far
when everything I do seems marred.
In the whole state,
I bet anyone couldn't get a much worse grade.
I can't retake the test, "too late."
I wonder if I'll ever get a good job that pays.

With you, it's never good enough
because you expect way too much.
All of this is valuable stuff
but you think it's nothing but junk.

Why would you set up a curfew?
How could you even have the nerve to?
Lock me up in this small, cramped room
and you expect me to respect you.
I'm never going to do drugs.
I can't carry money, or I'll get mugged.
I can't show that I want to be loved.
If I'm not me, is that good enough?

Missing

Will you ever know?
Don't you ever feel something missing?
Don't dare answer no.
I can tell you feel something missing.
Isn't something missing?
My days are spent wishing
for this emptiness to be filled
but the vastness only seems to build.

I know your soul aches
and you know there must be something more.
I feel your heart break
when you're not sure what you're looking for.

You don't understand
how much it hurts to be without you.
My heart breaks again,
all I want is to just be with you.
It's a lot harder than it seems.
I know you don't get what I mean.
When I look inside, it's difficult to find
what it is I need just to feel complete.

MY BIGGEST FEAR

Listen to the words I speak.
I'm begging you please,
let me get some sleep
and stay with me, don't leave.

I don't know what I have to do
just to get through to you.
I guess I'll never understand,
just tell me what's wrong, I'll help anyway I can.

Teach me how not to care
and not to notice when you're not there.
Somethings I might never learn
and my soul will be left to burn.

You make me feel so insecure.
My emotions left to stir,
not sure of exactly what I feel.
Some wounds take very long to heal.

I don't know why
you can't just tell me.
Please don't say bye,
I just want to see...

Why is it so hard?
Why are you constantly falling apart?
I want to help you
but you don't want me to.

I'm left alone here,
brokenhearted my dear.
My biggest fear
has left me in tears.

My biggest fear
is now what is real:
you all alone
and losing self-control.

THOUGHTS OF FAILURE

Wasted tears thrown in the garbage.

Pain running to me in a rampage.

Tugging on my heart.

Tearing my insides apart.

Feed my heart to the rats.

Throw my soul in the trash.

I need to get out of this place.

I need to be far, far away.

Thoughts of failure sinking deep inside.

I don't know how much longer I can hide.

I'm losing all of my pride

and no one is on my side.

When she falls, I want to be the one to catch her

but right now, I'm under too much fucking pressure.

It's not even cold but I'm shaking to the bone,

'cause I'm so scared of her leaving me all alone.

What's good of a CD that only skips?
What's good of a heart that's split?
What's good of this bible if it's bullshit?
What's good of a knife if it won't slit?

My friend is going through a breakdown,
but I'm dealing with it all somehow.
Life just sucks lately.
Everybody hates me.

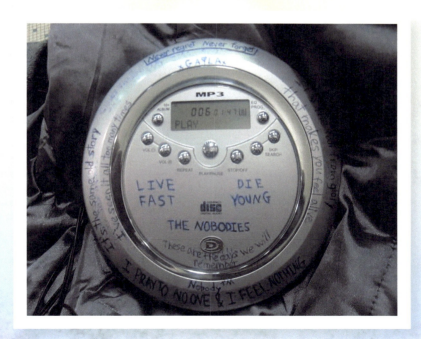

A Chance For Us

Just trust me, you'll be safe with me,
I won't let anything hurt you.
Come running into my arms
and I'll take all your worries
and throw them away for you.
I'll take away anything that hurts you.
I'll hurt for you.
As long as you're smiling,
I'll be smiling too.
I only want to hold you
and to keep that smile on your face.

The reason I get out of bed every morning
is to work up the nerve to talk to you.
Staring at you when I can
and when you look back, I look away.
I'm too embarrassed to say what I should say.
I fear to hear the answer I don't want.
Now there you are,
walking down the hall...
coming toward me, but not exactly,
then you pass by.
I just wonder why.

Just tell me... please tell me
that there's a chance for us.

Freak

How much longer until all this pain finally goes away?
When will things finally feel okay?
How much longer until someone really cares about me?
How much longer do I have to believe?

Inside I am empty.
Outside I am ugly.
They call me freak.
No one likes me.

People look at me in such disgust.
I am the one you just can't trust.
I'm sorry this is who I am.
No one will ever understand.

I'm always going to be alone.
All alone, left in the freezing cold.
Doors shut and locked in my face.
There's no place where I am safe.

My fingers smell of rust
from these rings of the dirt.
Why does this love
always bring hurt?

Always deserted,
so imperfect.
Is my happiness
even worth it?

A Bad Example To Kids

So I guess I'm not good enough for you,
or the rest of the "popular" group
but I hope you know you're beautiful
even though your insides are gross
I never wanted you to hate me
or to scare you away
but I can't change the way I feel.
So, what's the big deal?
Why am I the big freak?

God's the one who made me.
He made me this way,
so I guess he wouldn't want me to change.
So I can suffer, and he'll laugh from above
cause of the different way I love.
None of you have seen me cry,
you don't know what it's like to bleed from the inside.
Those sick, twisted butterflies,
I wish they would all die.

So, I guess I'm not human
because my heart is ruined.
There's nothing right about me.
I'm completely wrong.
I am a big mistake.

I should take my life away.
Don't try this at home.
It's a bad example to kids.

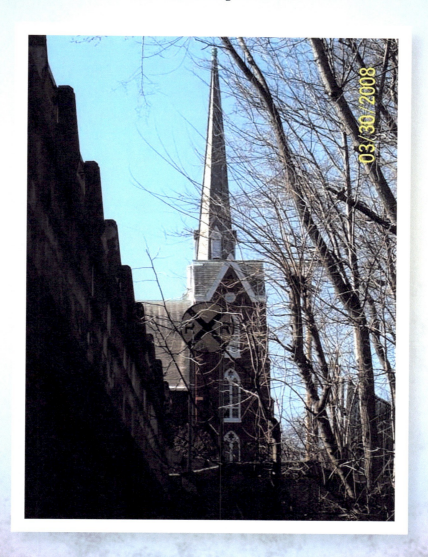

Not Fair

Why can't this country be truly free?
Why does everything come with a fee?
Why can't we all just work together?
Wouldn't compassion make things better?

I don't believe in God...
does that make me goth?
My heart is from the dump...
so now I'm a punk?

"Can't fight love." Is that saying real?
How do you think the LGBT feel?
"God loves us all." Is that true?
What if the sinners don't want him to?

I get inspired at different times.
It shouldn't even matter if I rhyme.
Even if I'm not able,
don't dare stick me to a label.

MESSED ME UP

I'm in love with you
and I'm in lust with you.
I wish you would treat me right
but I guess that's just life.
There's a smile on my face
but a frown in my eyes.
I wish I never met you in the first place.
I wish I could make up my mind.

You messed me up.
I wish I didn't want you so much.
Please go away.
I don't even want to think of you today.

When I think of you, I get lost.
I wish I could ignore your calls.
Instead I just fall into your arms.
I'll never get you out of my heart.
I feel like I'm buried alive.
It seems like I'm drowning inside.
I wish I knew what it was... about you that I love.
I'll always be... stuck in your penitentiary.

DEAR BEST

I love you.

No one else cares about me the way you do.

I wish you were here now.

Without you close to me, I get so down.

Nothing else matters to me.

It's crazy the way I want you so desperately.

I know life will get better.

I constantly daydream of our future together.

This is more than just a simple crush.

It's sweet when I tell you cute things and you blush.

My heart is drained from this pen,

and I know by the end of this, your cheeks are all red.

I know my love won't decay.

I promise you that I'll stay.

One more thing I have to say.

You're the only one in the world

that can make me feel this way.

THREE WORDS

I miss you.
Three words I can say
without confessing my love away...

Like you care.
At the show tonight,
I hope you're having fun without me.

Do you know how crazy you make me?
Every second I think about you,
wondering what the chances are
that you're thinking of me too?

I feel alone, left out
and full of so much doubt,
doubt of me being happy.
You're all I need to smile.

I love you.
Three words I must say,
I need to confess my love away...

A Waste Of Time

You say I'm cool and all

but I can't be seen when your friends come around.

You say you don't hate me at all

but you avoid me like I'm the biggest freak in town.

So, what's it going to be honey?

Should I stay or should I leave?

Should I consider this a waste of time?

Am I just a lesson you had to recognize?

I've been there when you needed me.

I'd do anything just to keep you happy.

Tell me what it is... you're afraid of,

tell me who it is... you really love.

You told me you love me

then you broke up with me.

My heart has shattered,

none of this mattered.

Why did I love you so much?

You gave me nothing but cuts.

Cuts on my heart.

Cuts on my arms.

There's A Fence Between Us

Something has happened
deep down inside.
I'm not really sure
but I don't feel alive.

My heart has shut down.
I can't feel anymore.
Lost all thought, staring down
on the dusty, dirty floor.

I can't feel.
It doesn't make much sense.
I know I need time to heal
after you built this fence.

This never-ending fence between us,
it will never disappear.
Only you could take it down
and get rid of this fear.

The fear to live.
The fear to die.
The fear to finally confess
all of my lies.

Just trying to impress you
but I'm bad at it, I know.
It's too late now,
and this heart needs to be sewn.

This fence you've built
is now surrounding me.
I'm stuck forever
unless you want to be back together.

Now come back to me.
I know you can't resist me.
Open your eyes and you will see
how much for you, I will bleed.

I Want To Die

This has become way too much.
I can't take it anymore.
This pain is going crazy.
No one can save me.

It's perfectly clear to me now,
happiness is weaker than sadness.
Nothing will ever be the same.
Even this pain is going insane.

I've never felt so hated.
No one cares at all.
Would anyone cry if I died?
Would anyone even mind?

All the love in the world is withering away.
All the smiles are disappearing.
The rain bangs on my head
and the sound of thunder wants me dead.

Every night I think of her.
Every night I can't sleep.
She's the only one who ever cared
and right now, she's not there.

Living in this broken family,
nothing will ever be perfect.
In this world, hearts are shattered.
Some lives don't even matter.

Every day we follow the same fucked up path,
turning down every chance to make a change.
People choose their fucking pride
over these innocent lives.

All alone inside this room,
no one cares about the weapon in my hand.
I don't know how much longer I can stay here.
My hopeful future is getting so unclear.

Only one person really cares
and I need her here so bad.
I am screaming inside.
I want to die.

AN HOUR TO LIVE

I'm going to die before the year ends.
My heart is already dead.
Who on earth can live without their heart?
I can't stay far apart.
What could you ever expect from me?
I can't do anything perfectly.
I feel like I have an hour to live
and I'm getting so bad at this.

I wish I could choose who to love
but life's not that easy.
Blame the fucking asshole above
for creating me.

It's 11:01,
the end has just begun.
59 minutes left
before my final breath.
So this is it for tonight.
In the dark, the pain shines bright.
Holding onto a dream that won't come true
is what God wants to put me into.

PANIC ATTACK

I've tried to just ignore
these things and focus on what I'm living for.
It's so hard and I'm not sure
if I can go on anymore.

I just need someone I can relate with,
anyone who understands this.
Something that will help me sleep at night,
make me believe I'll be alright.

Panic attack, striking inside.
Shaking in fear, I'm not alright.
Scared to live and scared to die.
I don't even know why.

I'm scared to live.
I can't get rid of this pain.
I'm scared to die.
Say goodbye to what kept me sane.

The light slips away from me.

I can no longer see.

I must go to sleep.

I'd never give up on you

but you gave up on me.

AFRAID

So afraid to live,
so afraid to die.
I don't know how I've survived.
I've come so far
and things are even more hard.

I don't know what to do.
I don't know how to get through.
I wish I could disappear,
just get away from here.
I can't handle this fear.

I can't sleep,
finding it hard to breathe.
It seems like the end is near
and all I can feel is this fear.
I'm going crazy here.

Starting to breathe heavy,
and I'm not at all ready
for this new day.
I'm just way too afraid.
I'll never be okay.

There's too much stress,
my mind is a total mess.
I can't handle life.
I'm going insane.
I can't take in the pain.

I wish I could calm down,
all I hear is my heart's pound.
Will I make it through tonight?
Will I ever be alright?
Will life get better?

Will I be forever
unable to put it all back together?
I should put down this paper and pen
and try to go back to sleep once again
because it's a fucking school night and it's 2:34am

What You Want Me To Be

Stupid and ugly
are two words to describe me
but nevertheless,
you know I couldn't care less.
Sorry the blood rushes slow to my brain,
it's too busy pouring out of my veins.

What's right for you isn't the same for me.
Could I do anything to make you see
that what's right for you isn't the same for me?

I'm not going to conform
and try to reform
to what you want me to be.
You might as well go away,
I'm never going to change
to what you want me to be.

Get the hell away,
won't do your demands today.
I've got my own issues,
I don't need any more from you.
I guess it won't ever matter to me
that it isn't what you want me to be.

How Could I Forget You?

Some scars take years to heal and some never do.
I guess I can't blame myself for still being attached to you
after what we've been through.

It's strange how in the past few months,
I've noticed a change in myself in the things I say and do.
I've noticed that I'm sort of like you.

Do you really believe we'll be together forever?
You promised you won't ever push me away again
and you know I never will
but does that mean we'll always be happy together?

It's just too hard to let go of you.
It's like loving you is keeping me sane.
You are a reason to live.
It's hard to explain but it's kind of like
if I let go of you – I'm letting go a part of me.

The hardest part is being miles away from you
but it's amazing how our love can still pull through.
It seems like you're in everything I see.
You're nailed in my memory
and in my mind, I think of you all the time.

You've made my heart burst; you've made it shut down.
You've made my heart melt and you've left it to drown.
With all these things that I've felt,
how could I forget you?

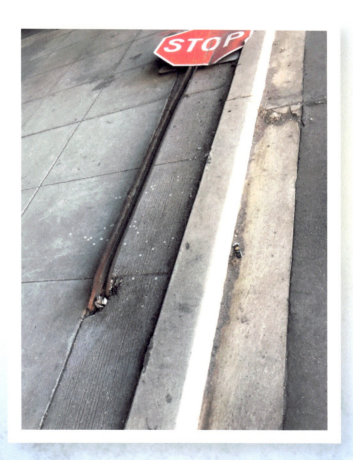

NEVER AGAIN

Crying uncontrollably.
Losing all my sanity.
Now nothing is left of me.

I should've fucking known
you'd leave me here alone.
You always lift me up
just to drop me back down...

And leave my heart to drown,
drown in its misery.
Dying in its own puddle of blood.

I thought you cared.
You're nothing but a fucking liar.
Block you from my mind.
Rip you off my heart.

Erase you from my memory.
Now you mean
nothing to me.

You've killed me on the inside.
Now I'll finish it off outside.
I thought you cared.
It's over. Forever. Never again. Ever.

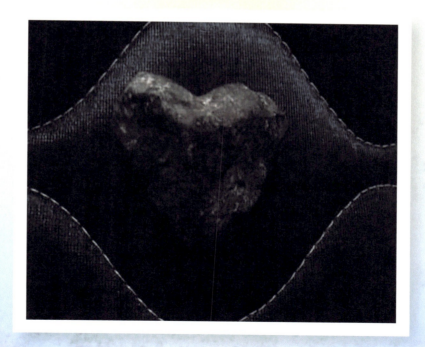

Air Is A Need To Breathe

How do you think this helps?
Let me live by myself.

You think if you send me to this place,
I can be okay.
You'll only worsen the pain.
I just want to be left alone.
I would be better being on my own.

I just want to be me
but you don't like my real face,
so you send me to this place
thinking I could change.

You only make me go insane.
You don't know how to ease this pain.

I'm sick of wearing this mask
and pretending to bask
in this life I do not like.
I can't live a lie for the rest of my life,
so I took off the mask.

You all gasp and scolded me to put it back on.
I can't stand it anymore,
this pain deep down in my core.
I'm not even sure what I'm living for.

You can't own the air I breathe,
unless you want me to suffocate.

Air is a need to breathe.
Let me grow up to be myself.
It's not wrong just because my direction is different.
Maybe... since you can't accept me for me,
I should just leave... tragically.

If you want me to be happy now,
then just let me die.
Maybe you'd see how much happier
I'd be just being me.

I'm your child,
not your fucking property.

Wait (I'm Coming)

I can't stand to see you like this anymore.
I want to save you now but I'm not sure how.
You deserve so much better than the life you have.
I see you... and I see you're trapped,
and drugs are all you have.

You need more... you should have so much more.
People say I shouldn't be so obsessed with you
but I can't help but have pity on you,
and all I ever do is worry about you.
You're so important to me,
and I can't stand to see you
beaten, defeated, and left so mistreated.

Let me be your new drug.
We shall call it love
and I will take your pain away.
You're trapped in such a deep, dark hole.
I reach my hand out and I promise I won't let go.

I won't leave until you're finally out.

I can't leave unless you're safe and sound.

I just can't live if you're not around.

I'll wait for you.

I promise that I'll wait for you,

so please hold on.

I'm coming to get you so please wait for me.

Feelings VS Instincts

I think it's truly time for me to let go.
This hurts me so much more than you'll ever know.
I really need to do this for myself.
It's time to let go and find someone else.

You once said I was the only reason you were still alive.
It sucked me into believing I was responsible for your life
and I hope you know you've completely lost all of my trust.
I hate myself for having hope and holding onto us.

And no, we can't even be friends
because this really has to end.

All the cuts that I have made
have healed up and gone away.
All the memories are fading
of every second I've wasted.

I've wasted almost a whole year on a fucking liar.
I wish I could set your pathetic life on fire.
Every dumb second I'd think of you and how you were doing.
I didn't notice anyone else or my life you were ruining.

I've learned a very important lesson from all this,
and I'm warning you now, don't follow your heart kids.
The heart knows what you want, the mind knows what you need.
I know I love her but it's for the best if I leave.

Dear Heart

I fell asleep singing our song.
I had nightmares all night long.
I woke up when I fell off my bed.
I finally woke up when you pushed me off the edge.
I woke up with the biggest hole in my chest.
What did I do to deserve being pushed off the ledge?

It just isn't fair
the way life goes on,
without being able to catch a breath
or understand why things went wrong.

Agonizing sorrow haunts my soul,
it haunts with these deadly thoughts.
I've spent these cold nights alone
forgetting what I was taught.
I don't know, if I should let her go.
I'm not sure, if I should stay with her.

I keep getting flashes of memories from last year.
The only feeling is the bitter fear.
My stomach squeezes and tears start to form.
I'm left alone, cold and so torn.

I see no color but gray.

My head thinks of nothing but you.

I just hoped you were still alive this day.

I didn't care of what I was going through.

Now my life is changing for the better

and I'm not going back to the past, never.

Dear heart,

you owe me an apology for reacting so emotionally.

Now I'm locking you up, you've lost all of my trust.

No one is to come in. My love's flame is now dim.

Understand

There's this note I want to give you
but I'm just too scared to.
I know you don't care anyway.
I care a whole lot but hey,
I'm trying to get this out to you
that I hate being alone
and my heart feels like a stone.
It won't stop sinking.
I wish you could understand.

I'm thinking about you too much.
My heart melts when I feel your touch.
I know you don't feel the same.
This is going nowhere but hey,
I'm trying to get this out to you
that I wish we were alone
and I want you as my own.
I can't stop thinking.
I wish you would take my hand.

I get so nervous around you.

My heart starts pounding when you're in the room.

I like your clothes style and your cute smile,

your dark eye lined eyes put light in my world.

Your voice is the only thing that I ever hear.

I know you don't feel the same way back

and that gives me so many heart attacks.

My heart is trapped in your hands

and I don't think you even understand.

My Heart Bleeds

Thanks for helping me get over an ex,
but now you're the one stuck inside my chest
and now your voice is repeating in my head,
listening to every word you had said.

You have so many other friends,
you don't need me to boost your self-confidence.
I'm sorry for not being strong enough for you
but I'm just too weak to have this pursue.

So go on feeling alive every day,
you don't need a hurt soul like me in your way.
Just know that people would die to be with you,
I know that I'm dying without you.

I'm dying for you; I'm crying as I breathe you in.
You don't even notice; you can't see me.
Every second you're near,
my heart bleeds.

Separate Ways

Don't rely on me to make you happy.
I can't put up your self-esteem.
I am just too weak.
Sorry I couldn't be prettier.
Sorry I can't be cool enough.
I'm torn apart by the ending of love.

If you ever took the time to look deep in my tired eyes,
maybe you would find
all the tears locked behind,
all the secrets I keep inside.
I don't believe in love that lasts forever.
I don't believe I can hold myself together.

I can't any longer.
The words you say are so much stronger.
They tear apart everything in me.
I don't care much about the way others differ
but I care about you.
I want to know about everything you've been through
to see if you bleed like I do.

Now I am walking behind you, you can't see my shadow.

The farther you are from me, the more I feel hollow.

There's a split to where we're going.

I try to get your attention by saying hey,

but I realize we should just go our separate ways.

CUPID'S ARROW STOCKED FULL OF POISON

Your voice rips through my insides.
I wish so bad you were mine.
It's so overwhelming thinking back on it.
I never know what to do or say in the heat of the moment.

Thinking about this makes me want to cry
but, how can I?
Your cute face in my mind makes me smile
but I'm vile.

The venom bursting from your eyes
gets aimed straight toward me.
The bitterness of your eye movement
reminds my heart there is no we.

The venom from your eyes
strikes my heart in stinging pain.
I try to run away for my heart's life
but I trip and my ankle gets sprained.

Now I can't go anywhere,
all I can do is look at you
knowing that you don't even care.
What else am I supposed to do?

I wish there was some way
that I could let you know,
I want to take your pain
and let it all go.

At least bury it all inside me.
For you, I'm more than willing to bleed.
This is not just a crush anymore.
I let this develop in my core.

Hearing your voice makes me fall in deeper
and the fall is only getting steeper.
I know I have no chance with you,
so sucking in the pain, I try and limp away.

"Amazing"

I just can't believe she's really over me,
everything we had doesn't exist at all anymore.
I lost something to live for.
I need to move on
but unlike her, I cannot forget the past.
I cannot forget everything I thought we had.

It all stopped in a change of heart
who was locked to someone new.
She threw me away and tore us apart.
She still tears me apart
every time she talks about him
and how much greater he is.

No matter how strong you love someone,
something always gets fucked up
and someone gets left alone to cry.
Freezing cold in the dark, all alone,
just constantly asking why
and when will my love for her end?

So I can move on with life
and forget the blood stains on this knife
and cherish that I am alive.
I once felt like I could jump up and fly
but now I can hardly crawl.
I guess I'm not so "amazing" after all.

Betrayed

You have those friends of yours
that care about you more than life.
They'll help you when your heart is sore,
they'll stick by you in your strife.

I once had a best friend
but now he's got everything,
a girlfriend and self-confidence.
He doesn't need me anymore.

I'm in pain but it's not like you care.
I'm just telling you so you're aware.
The times you said you'd always be there
are now just forgotten in the air.

I can now feel just how bitter and numb I've become
and how much I don't even care for my own self.

I'm so used to being called names
and people trying to offend me.
Trashing me like it was a game
and no one trying to defend me.

Don't leave your friends behind
even if you can't see through the smiles and lies.
They're screaming deep inside
how much they need you; they need you.

THE SAFE SIDE

I am alone
and that's the way it's going to stay.
All by myself.
I don't need anybody else.

I don't have any real friends.
They all insult me and call me names instead.
They all fucking take me for granted.
I hope I sound selfish.
It'll just make me more worthless,
just another of the many reasons why I should be dead.
It's just past 1am,
this silence will make me go deaf.

These annoying memories in my head.
I swear I could be happier,
I swear I could be dead.
I already am dead inside,
I'm so numb, it's unbelievable.
Please don't ask me how I am or how I feel
because I don't fucking care.
I don't care about myself.

I wish there was a way I could die,
no one needs me anyway.
I'm just that girl in your class
hiding behind a happy mask.
I'm just a girl walking past.
I'm a girl walking in circles.
I never learn from my mistakes,
a never-ending darkness of pain.

I'm so useless.
My life is meaningless.
I offered love
and I get treated like a freak.
I tried to be important, to be special
but I'm no more than the dust in the corner.
I just wish I meant something to someone.
I wish someone wanted me to live.

I wish I had something to live for.
I'm so used to being pushed around
and people turning me down
that I've locked myself up.
I can't open up.
I can barely speak.
I don't have any self-esteem.
This is all I know how to be.

Everyone loves destroying me,
you all team up against me
and I am so good at holding back my tears
and faking my smiles.
On my heart, there's an ice pack.
Numbing it till it turns black.
I'm sticking to the safe side
so my emotions must die.

2008/12/19

FOR THE DEAD

I'm tired of being pushed around.
I'm sick of being pulled to the ground.
I just want to feel alive
but living here, I can't.
I can barely survive.
I don't have any room to breathe.
I don't have any privacy.
I'm always getting interrogated.
I'm always ending up frustrated.
I'm stuck alone and agitated.

I know what it's like to be heartbroken,
how it feels like your soul has been stolen.
So empty inside, so vacant in your eyes,
how you would lock your heart up
because now you can't trust anyone.
You hope no one will ask you how you are,
too scared to tell them you're falling apart.
I'll hide out in my room and lay on my bed.
The days bleed together until my life's end.
I'll let my friends and family think I'm dead.

Writing these words really save my life
and I hope I can save whoever can relate.
Don't give up, even if you're dead inside.
Hang on because suicide isn't anyone's fate.

Wow

I love how you locked our lips,
right when I least expected it.
It was my first kiss.
I won't be forgetting this.

It probably wasn't a big deal to you.
You probably don't care as much as I do.
I think of the past so often,
I can't help but get lost in.

I wish you would kiss me again,
how about a one-night stand?
Oh please, just one more kiss.
Nothing's wrong with being friends with benefits.

"We're just friends"
is the last thing she said.
"Nothing more, nothing less."
I guess this is for the best.

I wonder if there will ever be a day
someone comes up to me to say
"I'd be so lost without you right now"
or anything for me to reply with "wow."

Whoever it is that I'm waiting for,
whatever it is that could heal these sores,
I just want you to know, without this hope,
I'd be long buried down, six feet below.

And Again, I Fall

The things you said
an hour ago
are still stuck in my head,
just so you know.

I can't let this happen again.
I won't let this build up so easily.
I see a hope in your eyes
and it terrifies me.

Do you know what it feels like being alone?
No one who understands when you're on your own
because I'm so destroyed inside,
I let my emotions die.

Now my emotions are dead
so I won't get hurt again,
but the words you've said
are bringing me back to life again.

I wish I had a pure heart to give
but it's been torn from my ex-girlfriend.
Now I'm scared to start over
and I'm scared to get closer.

I won't forget where I've come from.
I'll never forget where I've been.
I don't know what you have done
but I'm trusting you, my friend.

THE IRONY OF LOVE AND DRUGS

Kill these butterflies in my stomach.
This bullshit is making me sick.
I hate this stupid crush,
just talking to you makes me blush.

Get my head out of this love,
love is like being on drugs.
I have better things to do
than to waste myself on you.

She won't like me back anyway,
only friends is the way it'll stay.
I won't get my hopes up.
I won't begin to trust.

I won't let her in.
I won't forget where I've been.
I won't forget where I've come from.
I won't forget why I went numb.

Life is struggle. Love is war.

This is another infected sore.

I will end this battle before we both get worse,

before we both get ill and end up in a hearse.

Get off, stop weighing down my heart.

Get out, I'm not letting this start.

This just hurts too much.

Love, I've had enough.

THE PAIN OF REALITY

I'll never stop crying over this.
Without her, I feel so meaningless.
I feel like my life has no purpose.
I fell from the sky into the ground
and now I'm trapped beneath the surface.

I know that I will love you
for as long as you let me.
I know that I can't get through
without your friendship with me.

All day I think of everything you said
and I laugh and smile, lost in my thought.
The memories repeating in my head,
I can't deny the happiness you've brought.

It breaks my heart in two
to realize the truth.
I need to get over you.
It's okay if you never love me ever again,
just promise I'll have a spot in your heart until the end.

WHY I'M HOLDING ON

Keep your arms around me
as we lay on your bed together.
Hold my hand so tightly,
just let this moment last forever.

I can't look in your eyes,
I would just start to cry.
I wish I could tell you how beautiful I think you are,
but every time in mid-sentence, I want to fall apart.

You are my sun when clouds fill the sky.
You hold me close, every time I cry.
When I'm upset, you make me laugh.
You help me forget the bad in the past.
When I am weak, you try and make me strong.
Don't you see yet? You're why I'm holding on.

Remind me of how much I mean to you.
Promise you will never ever let go.
Remind me of all we have been through.
How can you forget and let it all go?

Your hand caresses my cheek,
you make my body so weak.
You kiss my forehead and say it's okay
but it's not because nothing will never change.

EVERYTHING THAT I HATE

Please don't hate me, it's not my fault.

If I could choose, I would not be alive at all.

For 3 years, I was so alone, surrounded by homophobes.

Now I'm here, losing a friend because of my sexuality.

Losing a great friend because of my personality.

Left alone again, to deal with my reality.

Have you ever been everything that you hate?

Every day I look in the mirror and remember that I'm gay.

Have you ever just wanted to fucking die?

Every morning I lay in my bed and acknowledge my insides.

Every day, I got evil stares in the hallway.

Every day, same routine, I knew it wouldn't stay.

If it did, I wouldn't have made it to today.

My only friends are what kept me sane.

I'm so grateful for every friend I make.

Every "I love you" is a bit of confidence I take.

I take it to try to build myself up.

In 3 years, I have learned so much.

I've learned more on how to survive than succeed.

Now I know how to react whenever I bleed,

and now I know the things I truly need.

I need to just be happy and feel alive.

Live life to the fullest before I die.

Next time, I won't let ignorant kids take away my pride.

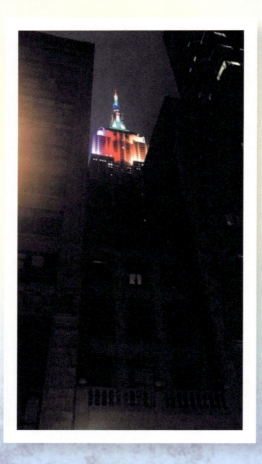

I Have A Loving Heart That Says Your Religion Is Wrong

Someone tell God I'm sorry.

He won't listen, he hates me.

When I was eleven,

I found out I would never go to heaven.

I found out God will never love me,

all because I'm a lesbian.

I found out something about myself,

I found out I was gay.

I almost died wishing I was someone else,

I never wanted to be this way.

Should I fake the butterflies and pretend that I like guys?

Should I be a heart breaker? Should I be a smile faker?

Like a child not wanting to play with a doll

with a missing leg or arm -

God rejects the people with fucked up hearts.

I'm sorry I can't be like everything you are.

You put me on this earth.
Please take me off of it,
or help me understand my worth
because I feel like a piece of shit.

So I'll ignore the way I feel,
block out the truth and what is real,
forget the meaning of my tears,
I've been doing this for years.

Box Of Memories

"We could hold each other.

I'll stop being a cutter,

as you see the marks they left behind.

Promise me you will still be mine..."

I never forgot those 3 lines

and the broken promise.

It's not that I miss this.

I just wish I could take it back.

You're a regret I'll always have.

Sometimes I wonder how I got so weak.

What ever made me believe and have hope in you and me?

Who are you now?

I haven't talked to you in years.

Have you forgotten me?

I'm nothing but evaporated tears.

I never was your only girlfriend,

that's when this should've been put to an end.

I should have run away to see if you would come after me

and if you didn't, I would just leave...

but why would I play hard to get

when I'm so obviously desperate?

You said sorry too quickly and I forgave too easily.

The poems you wrote about me
are long gone, shredded into millions.
The poems I wrote about you
are kept in my box of memories.

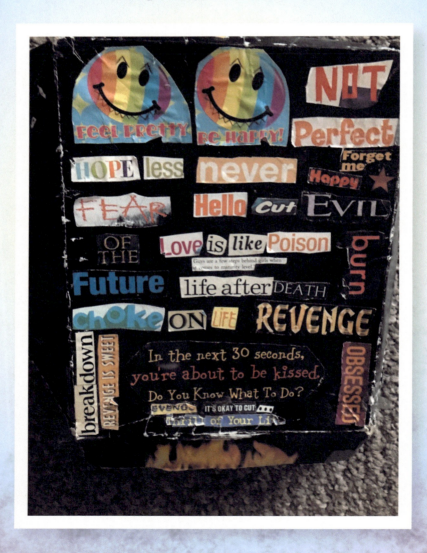

This Is Where I Don't See Myself In Ten Years

My hair is a complete mess.
I still haven't gotten dressed.
This is what's left of my weekend,
my weekend spent grounded.

Left locked up in these walls,
when I could be with my friends at the mall.
You don't understand shit,
you can't get me anywhere being strict.

You say I'm the one who doesn't get it,
you're the one that's so goddamn ignorant.
There's more than what the bible says about life,
that fucking book wasn't even written by Jesus Christ

Open up your fucking mind.
Do yourself a favor and define life.
Does it mean alive or just breathing?
Looks can be deceiving.

A guy with green hair and tattoos
could be a nice person who will help you.
A guy with a suit and shiny shoes
could be a person planning to kill you.

Sitting on the floor with my back against the bed,
I'm not going to abide by what you just said.
I'm going to keep fighting until I'm free
so just fuck off and give up on me.

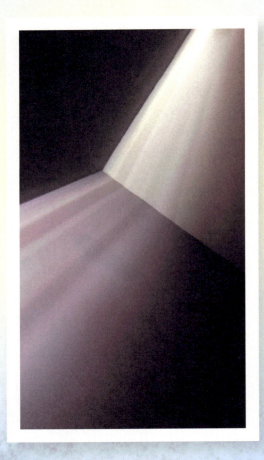

Never Understand

It's those weekend nights
and carnival lights.
Those precious moments
spent with my good friends.
For once I don't feel vile,
the hopefulness shows in my eyes.
My face shows a strong smile
and inside, I feel so alive.

I am so happy when I'm with my friends.
I feel like my life is making its amends.
I wish I could feel alive until my life ends
but it's people like you that will never understand.

So I don't get straight A's,
does that make me stupid?
Thanks for taking away
what makes life feel worth it.
Always find some excuse
to keep me under your control.
I'll never be like you
because you're a complete asshole.

CHANGE

My heart starts to freeze, and I just can't sleep.
Everything's changing.
What happened to everything?
The life I knew,
the pain that grew in me day to day.
The kids that were mean, waking up to the routine.
Everything has changed, I'm not at all the same.

All of the hate. Patience for fate.
The self-abuse. This is my muse.
Never been more alone, never felt more afraid.
Each heartache that caused tears,
I prayed for the end of my days.
It made such a horrible impact,
and I swear I'll never go back.

Now I see how things have changed.

Things will never be the same.

I see how all my past acquaintances have grown.

I see the change to what I know from what I've known.

Do I miss the shitty life I had?

I was so familiarized with the front and back stabs.

I should be glad.

The worst is over, and my blood still flows.

ANOTHER SONG TO BASE OUR LIFE ON

Hey dear, how do you feel?

How would you feel if I told you to go away?

Would that cut deep in your core?

Would you start up a chase after me?

Would you love me a little more?

I'll never forget what you did to me.

I can never go back to the way I used to be.

The blood I've bled,

the tears I've shed,

from the words you said.

I don't know why I tried so hard,

why I let this go so far.

There will never be an us again

and we're barely even friends.

I miss everything you used to be

but you're never coming back to me.

I'm going insane without you,

the fact that I can't breathe

doesn't make it easier to sleep.

You want me to come back too,

but what's the difference?

I don't keep your interest.

I've changed so much, look what you've done.

I'll never feel the same again for anyone.

The more you hurt me, the more I feel worthless.

Feeling loved by you, is it really worth this?

An End To This Emotional Confusion

I don't hate you; I hate loving you.

It's not you, not your fault at all.

You don't realize what I'd do, what I'd risk to be with you,

but you don't feel the same

and that's where it starts – the pain.

Feeling not good enough and totally worthless.

If I'm not beautiful to you,

I'm not beautiful to myself.

I don't care about the opinions of anyone else.

I wish I could see through your eyes into your mind

because you make me cry sometimes,

you hurt me and you don't even know.

Why am I so chained by these feelings?

Why won't they stop?

Why can't everything just be easy?

I suck at making decisions

especially ones that involve emotions

and you always get to me, right at my worst moment.

Just last night I felt so worthless,
and now this.
It's not like I have anything else for me.
I'm just scared of loving you
because you never feel the same as I do,
but I'm not myself without you,
I can't exist without your love.

WHEN EMBRACING THE SOLITUDE
IS ALL THAT'S LEFT FOR YOU TO DO

Fuck your stupid scene.

Do you understand the tortures of routine?

When you've felt it so long, day after day,

same feeling and it never goes away

till you just become used to it and kind of numb

and you never expect too much from anyone.

You see others who do nothing but whine

over stupid shit that's a waste of time.

While I keep my feelings locked inside

and my thoughts are trapped in my mind

and I wish I knew someone who actually understands

what it's like to be truly alone...

but at least I know I got my favorite bands

and this amazing world of being stoned.

Does anybody out there, care?

Entering class after class,
failing even more as the seconds pass.
I'm trying to live my life too fast.
After school, I have a detention
because in class I don't pay attention.
It's not like I'll ever learn my lesson.
Never mind the choices I'm making
and my insides that are aching
because this drama makes me sick,
sick to my stomach,
and sick in the top left of my chest.
It's complicated in my head,
all these thoughts after the next
from these feelings mixing around when I attempt to rest.

Does anybody out there, care?

The street I live on
is so dark and so long.
I'm walking alone in the middle of this street
staring down at my stupid, cold feet
on this dark, peaceful Tuesday.
I can hear the echoes of the highway
while listening to some songs in my head
and wondering what it's like to be dead,
wondering if I'll get anywhere in life

or if I'll somehow die tomorrow night.
The flickering streetlight on the shadows,
the muddy puddles are so shallow.
I love seeing all the beauty
of feeling empty and lonely.

THE ENDING OF THE BIGGEST CHANGE IN MY LIFE

Every girl I have liked,
I've given up on and continued life.
Every kiss that I give,
I've learned to let it go and just live,
but with you, it's different

Writing a love poem
for a girl I terribly miss,
writing a love poem
for a person who doesn't exist.
My life has changed thanks to a girl I've never met,
how much more pathetic could I get?

You said I've stuck by you through "everything"
and you don't want to lose me,
but with the way things are, starting to fall apart,
it feels like it was never meant to be,
and you know your time is running out
when all you can say are
remember when's and remember how's
and it feels like all our time is gone now.

Yesterday you said
this was the most pointless friendship you ever had,
did you honestly mean that?

Today you try to make me believe
that I mean everything to you,
which is honestly true?

You said I made you happier than anyone else.
I could feel my insides painfully melt.
You don't want to feel your true feelings
and with the way I've been lately,
this could be the ending of the biggest change in my life.

UNTITLED

Keep me up against the wall
if you want to know what's wrong.
Don't let go of my body
only if you still want me.

Push back my hair
and wipe away all my tears.
Say that you care,
say it softly in my ears.

A touch of your hand and now my legs are weak.
Hearing your voice leaves me unable to speak.
You've touched me in places unreachable.
and I love you in ways unspeakable

I'm Crazy Enough
But I'm A Goddamn Psycho When It Comes To Love

It's because of you that I'm going to fail an upcoming test.

It's because of you that at night, I never get enough rest.

I don't know if this is love or lust,

I do know I'm starving for your touch.

So, what do you think about

me taking a train to your town?

I'm being serious now,

I have it all mapped out.

A train straight to grand central in the city

and another to your town in New Jersey.

Thinking twice, I may sound a little crazy

but I would do anything for you baby.

I swear I would die

if it meant you would lead

and happier and healthier life.

Your smile is all I need.

I would walk through your burning house,
I'd burn alive to get you out
or I'll travel back in time somehow
and I'll turn things back around.

I'll fall forever in an endless, pitch black hole
as long as I know I'm saving your hurting soul.
I'll break every single one of my bones
if you could just please, stop getting so stoned.

I can't give up on you now.
My life goal is to save you somehow.
I know you're a lot better than this.
I hope I can save you with our kiss.

I believe in you so much.
I'll let myself die trying to save you from drugs.
I'll die to have your trust.
I'll do my best to save you with love.

THIS WAS A MADE-UP STORY AND IT PROVES, FANTASIES AREN'T AT ALL REAL OR TRUE

I miss the days when you used to be in such a great mood,

always leading me on and winding up in your bedroom,

falling faster and slowly in love with you,

confessing our secrets under the stars and moon.

Everything was so perfect; I had the world in my hands.

When I needed to talk, you were always there to understand.

We've saved each other's lives countless times and

now we're just washing with the tide like sand.

I feel like we're drifting apart.

We're both upset and things are getting so hard,

but we've been through so much, we've come so far

you're so much more than you think you are.

I don't think it's possible I could let you go.

You've opened my eyes to a world I've never known,

and there is no one else I know

who could help me feel not alone.

But I am tearing us apart,
this has been my fault from the start.
I'll do the first right thing in your life
and never talk to you again.

You'll forget we were ever friends
or secretly hope we'll talk once again,
while I secretly know we're both gone in the back of my head.

Yeah Right, Only In My Dreams

I have a scary, heavy feeling in my gut

during your time away, you won't miss me so much

and have you been avoiding me?

Whatever I did, I'm sorry.

What did I do?

I'm so confused.

What should I say?

I don't want you to go away...

but then again maybe...

it's for the best if we,

if we stop talking yet again,

I don't think we're meant to be friends.

But there are words I want to tell you face to face.

Daydreaming of getting closer with you in bed.

Please just promise me this isn't all a waste.

All these scars, memories carved forever in my head.

Do you ever daydream about you and me together?

I do... for hours and hours, for days and weeks on.

I'd like to believe that it'd be forever,

but I'm wrong, it's all for nothing, I lost you, you're gone.

"We'll Never Be Just Friends"

"I have my friends that are here for me too,
but that doesn't change things between me and you."
So what's going on now between you and me?
What if all this was never even meant to be?

We get into fights sometimes and stop talking,
but we're always okay again in the end.
Five years from now I see myself with you,
I just really hope you do as well too.

I don't know why but everything feels better when we're friends,
at least it doesn't feel like the world is coming to its end,
but I would do anything for,
for you to want me some more.

You leave me a voice mail saying you're bored and making soup,
every little thing you say makes me smile, you're so cute.
I won't lie, I know you've hurt me a ton of times,
but in the end, the only girl I want is you.

It's okay you don't feel the same way back,
I never did complain about that.
I was more than content, just being a good friend.
I just want things to be cool between us again.

It makes me feel like the most gorgeous girl,
knowing you think of me when I'm not around.
It makes me feel on top of the world,
knowing you want to help me when I feel down.

I need you more than a friend would,
I think about you more than a friend does.
I care about you more than a friend could.
Can't you sense the unconditional love?

I do not have a crush,
I just miss you so much.
It's alright that I'm jealous
of other girls you've done stuff with.

What is it about you that I love?
Why isn't being friends good enough?
I don't care about girls prettier than you,
not a single one of them know me like you do.

I wish I could just form a crush on them,
so I could get over you then
but for now, I'll rely on my friends
and the fucked-up days and nights we spend.
At least they'd never leave me at the end.

We'll Get What We Deserve

You said you hate liars.
Don't ask what's wrong.
I simply don't deserve to smile.
Fuck, here goes another poem.

I'm an asshole.
Yeah, yeah, I know
why I'm alone.

As a kid, I was always scared to do things on my own.
It's funny, I realize the past five years I've been alone.
It will stay the same in all my years to come.
I can't seem to let myself trust anyone.

I'm destroyed after what you did to me
but it's not even your fault.
I'm the dumbass who thought we were meant to be,
I'll remember this lesson I'm taught.

Getting over you
is something I'd like to do,
so if you'd be so kind
to please stay out of my mind.

Love is a deadly risk
that I will always inevitably miss.
I don't want to die so if you insist,
I'm afraid I must end it like this.

My Secret Fear Of You

I'm tired but I can't sleep,
something feels so incomplete.

You're pushing me away,
wanting me to let go
but I can't or else,
or else I might die.

I don't have anything else,
nothing else to hold on to.

I really don't want to let this die
but you have to help me win this fight
and I thought you cared
because you said you did.

I can't fucking see this.
I'm writing in the water,
the water that you caused.
It will drown everything we had for us.

These words raging on in my head,
these words will never be said.

I'm just too fucking scared.
I'm terrified that she secretly doesn't care,
it's a scar in our relationship.
I'll never know if she truly means it.

I will never be too sure when she says she cares about me
because in the past, she has deeply hurt me.
She's given me the first heartache I've felt,
the first ever heartache for someone else.

It just can't be the same
and she caused me to change.
I don't know how many times I can say that.
The closeness we had; I don't think it'll come back.

Here's another poem written about you,
here's another note I'll never give you
but in five years, none of this will mean a thing.
Just remember, you were once my everything.

WE HAVE TO TURN THIS DREAM INTO A REALITY

It's the way I constantly think of her when I least expect it.

She's just constantly in my head

because everything reminds me of her

and then I pretend I'm talking to her.

I get sucked into some fantasy world

and she's there with me

but I laugh

and snap back into reality.

Sometimes it gets really scary

that I can't even control what to focus on.

Maybe I need to stop thinking so intensely about it

but how do I stop this?

I can honestly say,

I can make anything to make me think of her.

Just the whole state of thinking itself

reminds me of her.

The thoughts occur the most
when I'm laying down trying to go to sleep.
Sometimes my imagination gets so real
and it feels like she's laying right there with me.
But I'm really into some far-off world,
some place... where our bodies are together
and we're talking and she makes me laugh
and I wake back into reality again.

It'll only take about 2 seconds till I'm with her again
and sometimes when I talk, my lips are really moving
and I fall deeper into the dream.
While I hear her voice, it's so soothing.
It seems that writing is my only good release
but I still need to show you these words
and for you to say it's all okay, you set the pain free.
If I didn't show you, they'd still follow and haunt me.

It hurts to face reality.
Reality is that she's so far away from me
but she's always there, mentally
and she's never left, emotionally.
Physically is my only need.
I need your body next to me
and that day when I get to touch you,
I swear I'll finally feel complete.

I Need Only Me

This fight could have been prevented

but you're taking me for granted,

and I'm fucking sick of it.

I do deserve better than this.

This has got to be put to an end.

She said she would call early,

but I guess she forgot me.

Even though I'm angry, I know how it'll end up.

I'll be saying sorry even though she was just busy

puking out her guts.

You won't tell me why you feel like hell

but you make it obvious in other places,

on social media, as if I wouldn't notice

Why does everything you do and say

make me want to write in such a pathetic way?

Just go out and get fucked up and forget me.

If you don't tonight, you will eventually. You don't need me.

Just give it a few more weeks, you'll get over me.

With tear stained cheeks, I realize the only person I need is me.

I am as real as real comes,
the only thing I hide are my emotions.
It's going to take more than three
asks to get the secrets out of me.
I need someone who will take my side
and not just give me the right advice.
Are you even ready to put up with this?
I'm scared she won't care
and then I'll just be crying the rest of the night
and probably for the rest of the week.
If I never talk to her again,
I know I will be for the rest of my life.
Days go on like a dead person's dream.
Now that she's gone, I feel so incomplete,
like something's missing from inside of me.

I'm sick of that melting feeling
of beginning to trust, to love again.
I'd rather attempt to die than tear these walls down.
Never shall I be so vulnerable again
but please don't leave, don't give up.
I'm sure there's a crack somewhere,
a weak spot to start from, so start from there.
Don't give up, prove how much you care
because I do need someone
but stay away, oh stay the fuck away,

because there's nothing in this world
that could scare me more than you getting sick of me
and I'd rather face my fears
with the slight hope of hopelessness,
than to be stuck with unfulfilled wishes.

LOVE ON DRUGS

All I have is a hope of meeting someone new.
I really hope I do,
but there's a part of me and there always will be
that never wanted to give up on you.
I'm trying to figure out
what's happened to you now,
wondering how can I
get out the girl trapped inside?

All your pores are pouring out
all your pain everywhere
and I just can't seem to get around,
now I'm stained and I care.
There is no such thing as hopelessness, only helplessness
and I've thought up a plan.
If you go through with this, maybe you'll finally get over it.
Start by taking my hand.

The human eye is too blind
to see inside, all the emotions you hide
but I bet I'll find some secret signs.
Don't tell me to move on
or get over it and forget it.
I don't want to feel like this
but one of us has to feel something.
Could this all really have meant nothing?

Nothing To Save But The Jaded Edge Of A Razorblade

Days go on as if a dead person's dreaming.
I'm completely losing everything.
I don't know what's happened.
What's happening to me?

I'm losing my innocence.
That's exactly what it is
and it feels just like
I'm losing myself.

Someone save me.
Don't let forgotten memories
be all that's left of me,
all that's left to save me.

I want to know what love really is.
I want to know how to live without it.
I want answers, I want them now
or I might do more than leave this town.

You said you'd never stop caring.
You said you'd always be there and
please just don't... don't go.
You said you'd never let me go.

I can't begin to sleep.
I'm in so much shock.
She used to care so much,
and now she's just stopped.

Everything is stinging me.
I'm taking in double the pain,
just knowing you feel nothing
because you feel nothing now from me.

I'll do all the crying needed tonight
since you won't even be thinking of me.
I wish you had a clue
of how much this really hurts.

Ripped Up

She said she needed me in her life.
I need her in mine too
but how is it possible to fix any of this?
This hurts a million times more than all the times
she hurt me while talking to her combined.
I need to talk to her, without her in my life,
it's such fucking torture.
I swear to God I'd give my life up,
if it meant she would never do a single drug,
take pills or even smoke a cigarette ever again
or even get a craving for any of them.
I hate this that much.

Now I don't know who she is,
the girl I ... I always miss.
She's the girl in my forgotten dreams,
in all of my blurred-out memories.
I hope she at least remembers me,
because sometimes I cry
and I don't know why or who it's caused by.
I'll just rip up this paper and let it blow in the wind.

The chances of me falling in love with someone that's better
is like her finding all the pieces of this ripped up letter
and actually bothering to put it all back together,
together again.

INNER STRENGTH CONQUERS ALL

I remember the days when I forgot how to cry,

but now it's all I ever do with my worthless time.

My dad says if one more time he sees my poems

scattered all over the corner of my floor,

he'll throw it all away.

Just throw me away.

You've proved me absolutely worthless.

Just remind yourself it could be a lot worse

and it's everybody for themself in this world.

Breathe real hard and real fast till you get a headache.

Squeeze your fingers so hard till you think they might break.

I hope she means it this time.

I might as well be repeating the above line

for the rest of my life.

Please don't talk to me

until you're drug free or at least mostly.

Just remind yourself it could be a lot worse

and it's everybody for themselves in this world.

I am content and I see a future for me ahead
and I'm not going to bring myself down ever again
to worry about somebody
that I don't even fucking need.
I know dreams can come true,
maybe not the exact way you wished for it to,
but it could happen to you.

2008/12/28

Sorries Won't Save Us Now

I guess it is pretty fucked up what happened to us
but I'll just keep reminding myself I have had enough.
Now listen here, I didn't fucking say I didn't care
but I really don't want to admit you're still everywhere.

I have every right to give you all of my hate,
you have no right at all to give me all the blame.
I guess you really are a worthless piece of shit,
your life's dead and I'm not going along with it.

I hope you miss me, and I hope it hurts
because it will for me with every word,
with every word I've written and will write,
I hope to everything you cry tonight.

If I dare start to stupidly miss you,
I'll remember the near death you put me through.
I'm not apologizing for what I did
because you deserved every last bit of it.

I hope you're happy, having pushed me so far away
I'm not coming back, just to get hurt more in my stay.
This time I'm running, running far, far away from you.
What could be as bad, as what you fucking put me through?

I hope you miss me, and I hope it hurts
because it will for me with every word,
with every word I've written and will write,
I hope to everything you die tonight.

A Bit Of Confidence

I don't know how the human race is still existing

but I guess when there's no way to die, you live.

I'm no scientist or future politician,

I'm nothing but another naive 15-year-old girl.

I'll doubt I'll be someone big and famous or change the world,

I don't even know if I'll live past 24.

I don't have those so-called real or best friends.

It's also illegal for someone like me to wed,

and my goddamn cuts take forever to mend!

The sun goes down and my room gets darker,

I want to write poems like I did when I was younger

but now this air has gone stale.

I can't properly inhale,

I can't breathe in anywhere.

I remember when my young mind corrupted with pornography,

I used to think sex seemed so painful and nasty

but now I've grown, and my hormones have changed me.

Touch me, fuck me or show me what love means.

I'm not totally a piece of trash,

here's something I think I may be good at.

Not everyone could be a good poet

unless they really wanted to be.

All we need is to keep going at it,

I think, or at least that's what I read.

Please, please, don't be confused and think I'm at all conceited
because I know how it feels when your insides are bleeding.
Internally, in a way you cannot see,
emotionally is just as damaging.
Just remember it's okay not to be okay.
Wake up to see another day.

After all these years, I've finally gained a bit of confidence
and it feels so great to be finally off that depression bench.

LIKE A DREAM

There's this girl I see
and she makes me so happy.
Now I don't want to sound sappy
but that is exactly
how she makes me feel.

I can't believe
all that you're doing to me,
it hasn't even been a week.
All that you're making me feel,
it's too damn good to be real.

You bring up my self-esteem.
Right now, I wish you were with me
with your hand in my hand,
with my hands all over your body.
I can't get enough of you baby.

You better never leave me
or I'll just cry endlessly.
Assuming lasting love isn't real
and this all was just a dream.
This all feels like a dream.

BEFORE SUMMER ENDS

I want to write a song
but inspiration's gone.
The passion is still there
but my mind doesn't care.
The night's feel extra cold
even though it is summer.
The distance between us
feels like thousands of miles.

I really thought you were different
but I guess I'm just not meant,
I'm not meant for a relationship yet
because everybody's a fucking liar.
It's times like these at the world's end...
are there any non-backstabbing friends?
"Is love real?" isn't even the question,
who cares when the world is on fire?

I don't mean anything to anybody.

Nobody will ever love me.

I'll just drown myself in the riverbed.

I'll make sure I die before summer ends.

Just forget me or pretend I don't exist.

I guarantee I won't be someone you'll miss.

Just forget me because I guarantee

I will not be missed and I do not exist anymore.

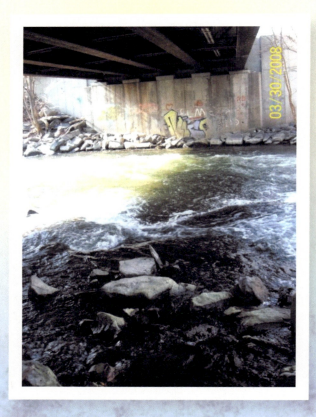

BETTER THAN ME

I bet she's not thinking of me,
as I'm crying.
I bet she's on the phone with Ashleigh,
as I'm dying.
I bet she's happy,
happy without me.
I miss her scent,
I wish I could touch her again.
I miss her taste,
I really wish I could go back to those days.

I really want to call her
and confess how much I miss her
but she wants nothing to do with me,
and she's made that so clear to see
I'm going to be alone forever.
There will always be someone that's better,
better than me.
I'm going to be worthless forever.
There will always be someone that's better,
better than me.

Every night's a series of awful dreams.

Every morning I feel again my heart being torn at the seams,

torn vertically and horizontally,

over and over and over repeatedly.

I wish I wasn't lesbian,

none of this would be happening.

I could be happier

if I never let her in.

Now how are things supposed to get better

when it seems like nothing can be fixed?

Everything's turned to shit

but keeping myself occupied

seems to keep you out of my mind.

It's all I have to save my life.

I've been keeping myself busy,

I won't wonder if you miss me.

I Am The Weakest Link

I've got one more day left,

till I can keep my promise

and put my life at its end.

My worthless life to its death.

You said it's not worth it

and you know me, more than anybody.

You told me all I am

and just how worthless my existence is.

You say I don't give a shit

but the real reason I'm not talking

is because I'm crying,

because I'm crying.

I'm wasting too much time,

on a love that's not mine,

on a hope that's always dying.

And if I never talk to you again,

would you even notice it?

I'm nobody you need,

please just let go of me.

You've lost your strength
and I am losing faith.
This is also getting stupid,
don't you think?
The days go by
like they don't even matter.
I ask myself why
and I start to wonder...

There's something wrong with everybody in this world.
There's too much medication needed on this earth.
The only reality I have is behind these eyes.
The only truth I know is that everybody dies.
What's the purpose of my existence?
The way I think is ridiculous
and overwhelmingly depressing.

I wish I knew what's causing me to feel like this.
I feel like I am truly at my weakest.
With vacant eyes, I lie on my bed.
Motionless, embracing my worthlessness.

SMILING

As the minutes get closer,
I'm getting more and more nervouser
and that's not even a word,
but these feelings are also absurd.
The feelings are coming back,
coming back little by little.
Feelings I've tried so hard to stab away,
they're coming back and making me shiver.

Imagining what could be
if only, if only we
were together for a night,
yeah for just one night baby.
Watching you sleep,
hearing you breathe.
There's nothing in this world
more precious I believe.

Smiling myself to sleep.
Smiling so hard, it hurts my cheeks.
Smiling so wide, I can't speak.
Love overflows inside me.

PROMISE

Every fight we get in
can make us weaker
but in the end, it's never the end.
We're only getting stronger.

You know we can always work things out,
we can talk and work out our problems.
We'll find a way to fix things somehow,
just open up baby, we'll solve them.

So please keep this promise
to never give up,
never give up on us.

Just open up, you know I care
and I'll try to always be there.
Just open up to me, you know I care so much
and I promise I will never give up on us.

UNREALISTIC DREAM

In my head, I am reaching out my hands
but there is nobody around to grab them
and put me back in the right direction.
In my head, I'm spinning in circles.
Everything's fuzzy but you're a pure picture.
You're not a blur in this distorted world.

Your face is so precious,
I'm scared I may break it.
Your existence is so cute,
I'm scared I may hurt you.
I'm sitting here writing,
you see me and question.
I say I'm not doing anything
but how do you see through this?

I feel much too sentimental
and you're far beyond gentle,
and isn't it so bad how
I am so vulnerable?
So tell me, what's going on with us?
I'm sorry I unintentionally tripped,
but now will you pick me back up?
Please help me up or I'll get crushed.

I'm thinking way too intense,
it scares me a little in my chest.
I feel so unbelievably blessed,
just being in your presence.
Your posture is so sweet and innocent,
I can't quite understand it.
All I know is I want it
so come on honey, give me it.

I am so high
that I can barely feel you from across the room.
Are you the love
that will help me feel the warmth of the sun?
Show me the sun, I'll bring you the moon
and the stars will show in between
for everybody else to see.
I am so lost in this unrealistic dream.

I wish it would work,
the way I play things out in my daydreams,
but I've learned my lesson,
I know these things won't happen to me.
I won't waste my time,
floating and hoping near the ceiling
because I sure damn hate
that terrible sinking feeling.

The things I just dreamed about
will never come true now.
I just jinxed myself.
Damn, I'm in for a letdown.

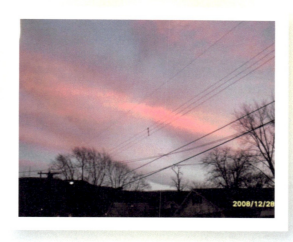

BEAUTIFUL BURNOUT

What would I do, to be able to
unsnap that bra from your back,
and slide my hands in your pants with ease
as I come from behind you.
Oh, just give me a chance please.
Let me touch your fragile body,
stare your fucked-up eyes into mine.
Let our hands intertwine.

What I'm saying is we should have sex.
You make me wet, just by looking at you.
After we get stoned, I'll make you moan,
you won't even know what hit you.
You don't know how hard I'd try
to keep your needs satisfied.
Have I written about you?
Honey, you haven't a clue.

I tried to win her over while being original
but it's not working
cause she already knows
that she's amazing
and beyond beautiful, beautifully burnt out.
As a matter of fact, she's stoned right now.

You're really nothing but a monster.
On the outside, you look innocent and sweet
but I see through your careless intentions from beneath,
with your demonic means
and the poison spewing on your lips.
Pity on all souls who fall into your grip.

I'm not sure if anyone else can
but I totally see through your lies.
I hope you're aware you need to work on
your pathetic, terrible alibis,
and it almost makes me want to cry
how hopeless you are on the inside.
I'm still trying to understand
what makes you the person you are.
Is anything fixable?
Are you just a falling star?
Do you even know that I care?
I don't think you see me at all.

UNDYING SENSE OF PAIN

All I'm aware of is my worthlessness.
I will end up just like my parents,
just motiveless and without a purpose.
I don't think I'll know true happiness.
Who can I talk to when I feel like this?
What is it like to have someone's best?
Why do I get so easily depressed?
How can I feel complete without something to grasp?

Everywhere I go, someone's holding hands with somebody
and I walk alone, fingers clenched to the palm of my hands.
Sometimes I look at the eyes of strangers walking by,
I'm just a meaningless figure passing through their lives.
There's a song my dad used to listen to
saying "someday, love will find you"
but you can't say everyone falls in love and gets married,
sometimes the love you get isn't always the love you receive.

I am writing these words in all honesty at age sixteen.
I don't know what it's like for someone to be in love with me,
maybe I'm just too young to know
but then how is everybody else so sure,
and so much more experienced than me?
There isn't a single word that could explain
or help you feel this undying sense of pain.

Isn't there more to life than living?
Do things really happen for a reason?
I don't agree this justly evens things out.
I wonder if I'll be just like the high population
of all the students in college
that kill themselves because they can't find help.
It's during this time when most people realize
they've got nothing going for them in life.
I'd rather walk towards the light.

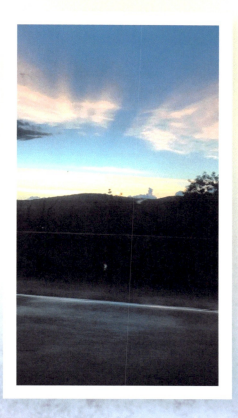

LET THE BLACKNESS TAKE ME IN

I don't belong here,
I never did.
Why has it taken
so long to realize this?
There's no future, love or hopes
in this homosexual 16-year-old.
This life is a complete tragic mistake
and this heart and soul can never be saved.

Goodbye to my friends
who will never know the impact they made.
Hello to my death
and the maggots that are waiting to be fed.

I'll find happiness amongst the deafening silence
and the peaceful blackness that will suck me in.
Unable to feel, see or even exist,
I want to embrace my only purpose.
My mind is being so serious.
It's time to see the end of everything,
not just true happiness.
Let the blackness take me in.

SOMEBODY

I can't hold this in any longer, I need to let it out.

In my head and heart, it's all slowly breaking down.

I've been single for over a year now.

There's no other lesbian like me in this town.

When I first fell in love,

it seemed like I was dying of so much happiness.

It was by far the most

amazing, unexplainable feeling

but it was forced to end too quick

and I've yet to feel that since.

I'm dying, wishing somebody could fall in love with me.

Somebody I can confide in all my secrets.

Somebody who can make me feel beautiful just by looking at me.

Somebody who will help me believe in myself.

Somebody who will tell me their whole lives

so I can feel secure enough to tell them mine.

Somebody who will walk by my side

and hold my hand everywhere we go.

Somebody who will look in my eyes

and tell me how much they care,

and will keep looking when I just can't anymore.

Somebody who smiles just hearing my name.
Somebody who will keep calling or keep following
even when I hang up or walk away.
Somebody who can make me feel needed.

Somebody I can call when I'm crying at 3 in the morning.
Somebody who will talk with me on the phone for hours.
Somebody who will let my tears dissolve on their fingers
and soak into their shirts.
Somebody who couldn't let me feel worthless
because I know I'm their world.
How could any of this ever come true?
I just want to die of happiness if I ever meet you.

"I've Witnessed Horrible Things From Beautiful People"

After all this time of thinking,
I've finally come to a conclusion.
Everyone I've shown affection for
has never felt the same towards me at all,
and it's too damn bad that now it's too late
because everything inside me has drained away.
Nothing to give and nothing I want to take
because all I'll be to them is a fucking waste.

It's been so long since I've shown an interest,
it's been even longer since I've received.
I know deep down I'm inexperienced,
there's just a fucked-up heart that continues to bleed.
I know it hurts really bad
when someone says they care
but then they take it back
and you try so hard to bear
but all you do is ask yourself
what is the point of this?

These nights are sleepless
and the dreams I do have are filled of
security, protection and love.
Sleeping forever doesn't seem like such a bad idea,

I'm just tired of waking up to the way I feel.

I can't face reality,

I want out easy.

Hopeless despair is all I see.

I am so sorry

but I admit to being weak.

I heard her say in my dreams

she's going to be here soon and she's going to save me

but I was only asleep.

I wake up begging to the God I don't even believe

to please find a quick way to kill me

and please just hurry

or bring someone quickly

or I don't know what's going to become of me.

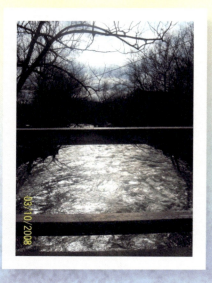

HONESTY

The grass and trees
are a perfect green.
The air feels so nice
and the clouds are pure white.
The sky is so blue
and today is beautiful.
Only thing is I really miss you.
I just want you to call
to make me tell you what's wrong,
for you to say it'll be okay
and say you still care about me.

Your voice is resonating in my head again,
telling me to tell you things I've kept hidden.
You know the word love
really means so much
so please tell me what you actually meant.
I care a whole lot Jess.
What if this was our last night alive?
Would you still hope we only remember the bad times?
Just like that, I can cut you out of my life
and it's okay, this is our last night.
Please tell me what's on your mind...

All I want is you to tell me
in all honesty
how you really feel,
but you won't
and I know
none of this is real.
You can't take back these words you've said
because they'll always replay in my head.
They'll always keep you in my heart,
no matter how far we are apart.
Do you want me to tell you how much I love you still
and describe how you're so fucking beautiful?
Believe me baby I will,
you're still the most amazing girl ever.
My head is resting in my arms, face down.
I wish there was a real way to let this out.

LOST AND FORGOTTEN

Leaving it all behind,
lost and forgotten in the back of my mind
feels just about right for tonight.
I'll let these unoriginal rhymes
write themselves one last time.

I'm not holding onto anything
but I hope you'll remember me,
like you were my everything,
and I'll know I never meant a thing.
Now I don't know what will be
but I've got the apathy to wait and see.

I just want to be sure to stay far out of your way
from you and your great future you are about to convey.
I wish you the best and true happiness
which I always thought you deserved from the beginning.
I don't think that I'll ever be blessed
with someone equal to or more caring.

Please believe... that I fucking hope you'll stay happy
more than I could hope for anything,
hope for anything ever again...
and it makes me mad that I mean that.
Maybe one day your intolerance will end
but you'll already be lost and forgotten in the back of my head.

LET IT GO

I hope you're happy
having forgotten all about me
and everything that happened between us
but I'll never see the ending of love.

I know you don't care anymore
this time I've really hit the cold, wooden floor
but the wood is splintering and breaking
I might just fall through.
You'll never see or even know of this writing.
I've written it all for you,
begging we don't have to talk everyday then anymore
because I just don't want to say we don't talk at all.

I'm never going to send this
because I know how it is,
you've been long over me,
I'll never start moving.
So just let it go and leave me alone.
Here's the solution, one we always come to
every time we get into a fight.
Let's stop talking and forget each other
because you don't care, and I don't either.
If I continue my lifestyle and just give it a little while
and tell myself that you don't give a shit,

I'll be over this.

Is this really the end?
I'm past the point of no return.
What a slow painful death
when thoughts of you still burn
and how you got me to believe
you cared so much about me,
yet you can drop me so easily.
I know now to you, I am nothing.

I always thought we were so close
but we were always so far
and what hurts the most:
you were my greatest love and mistake of all.

No, I don't hate you, you know I never could,
and yeah, I still care, I said I always would
but damn I am so mad, hoping you're fucking glad
and that you'll never try talking to me again.

Maybe there's even a chance you could forget my existence
and I'll be just fine sticking close behind my friends.
This is really the end.

STEP ONE: ANGER

I know we'll make it. I know we're destined.

You're the only one.

There's no one else I've ever loved.

Baby honestly, you're everything I've ever dreamed of.

I still think about you every night.

I want you for life.

I don't believe we're as broken

as you think we are.

It's been months since we've spoken

and your body is so far

but I still want you,

you and only you in my heart.

No one else could ever get inside

to the place I hide

that you know how to find

every single time.

I still love her, but she doesn't love me

and goddamn she's ruined it for everybody,

for everyone else who could even have a slight chance.

I just can't put myself in that situation again.

I'm trying to forget it all as best as I can

but I'll never get over this, I hope you understand.

Does she love you as much as I used to?

So I see you're happy, do you know I'm going crazy?

I haven't been myself and I'm getting worse lately.

Yeah, this is another note you'll never see.

I just hope you know the last time we talked wasn't me,

and I'm honestly sorry

for my pathetic reasoning.

Anger is all I can think of to let go of everything.

I can't tell you anything anymore.

I don't want it to seem that's all you're there for.

You don't talk to me either, you don't talk to anyone

and that's just our problem.

I'll open when you get broken.

I hate all these rhymes.

See how you cloud my mind?

I hope I bother you; you haunt me every night.

Sometimes I even still cry

but why would you care? Don't lie.

Just to put yourself up

higher than you already should be

but you don't need to hear my thoughts,

you don't at all need me.

So stop asking, it's just too much.

Stop caring, because I want to give up.

Just delete me, it's that damn easy.
Nothing matters to me but my friends anyway.
I don't care anymore what you say.
Don't you get it?
It's a desperate, pathetic, psychotic obsession.
Just forget me,
it's not like you ever met me.
I'm selfish and ridiculous
and every sentence is just more bullshit.
Every minute of my life is meaningless.
Someone show me a good purpose.
My head just doesn't care enough anymore,
with a rotting core
and an ego stomped on by my own shoes.
I want to die behind bolted doors
and without saying bye to you.

BEACON SUCKS

Beacon sucks,
so many skanks and smuts.
I'll never get with anyone
that's worth any trust.
Whatever, I don't give a fuck.
Why do you feel the need to be in a relationship?
Why can't you accept loneliness?
It only hurts a little bit
but I'm still alive with it.

School gets so depressing sometimes.
I just get so lost passing by all these different lives
that are probably so much better than mine.
Does anyone even understand my side?
I think I'm crazy sometimes,
and that's probably why I'm on no one's mind
but I'd rather not worry over another life.
This one is more than enough to think over at night.

Hearing that a girl likes me
really doesn't excite me.
It's actually slightly scary
wondering how things could turn out to be.
The songs she listens to on a daily basis
remind her of the same things,

or at least a person in particular
who blatantly hurt her.

I just need a hand,
a different perspective,
but no one understands,
I just don't want to live.
We still do the best we can
living a life we'll never understand
with holes in our hearts and weights on our backs
stronger than we can stand.

Don't Mess With Messes, Enough Said

She's not someone I should mess with
but obviously I am so desperate
and she makes me feel so special,
like maybe I actually matter.
Oh, I know I shouldn't bother
but I'm sick of being lonely,
although I'm scared to fill that hole in me.
I'm so used to the emptiness
that anything else will feel wrong.
Once she sees my craziness,
I know she'll be gone before long.
I'm independent but I can't mend my own head.
I can't deal alone with my own problems,
I smoke and drink instead.
She doesn't even know what I'm all about,
I'm plagued everyday with shame and doubt
but what if she has the key to help me get out?
I don't know now...

She doesn't even know what she's getting into.
She's just confused
and I need booze
because I see I've still got a heart to lose.
I've been single 17 whole months

and in this past year, I haven't shown any care once
but now she's messed my streak up,
that doesn't mean she'll easily gain my trust.
I know better than that,
thanks to all the times I've been shot and stabbed,
not literally, but mentally and emotionally.
I don't regret anything, but it still changed me
and I still believe it wasn't fucking worth it
so maybe in a way, I regret some things a little bit
because I'll never forget this stuff.
My head is still twisting and turning
from my mistakes I wish I could purge of
but I know there's nothing I can do about anything.

I'm so dirty and gross,
I shower like 3 times a week
and for days on, I wear the same clothes.
How can you say I'm beautiful?
My face is oily and covered in pimples,
imperfection is written all over.
Don't just say sweet things.
Don't use me as a rebound.
It's hard to believe anything,
I told you I'm full of doubt.
I will bring you down.
I wrote this all through 6th period

and every single line is serious.

It'd probably be best if you forget I exist.

I'm not someone you should mess with.

I'm aware I just totally flipped this around.

Do you see that I'm crazy and senseless now?

Just rip up this paper and throw it on the ground.

RIDING TILL WE DIE

Life is like a roller coaster,
so many ups and downs.
Some people just have it better,
some are farther from the ground
but either way, it'll just fly you into the end of your days.

No one is born into the body, brain
or life they want to be in.
No one has any control at all,
all you get is a bar.

You know what I say?
Fuck the bar and put your hands in the air
and fucking scream.
If you think the plunge is too much to bear,
remember nothing's what it seems.

Feeling the pressure fuck with your stomach and head,
you'll realize nothing makes you more alive
than the moments that want you dead,
and having survived the hardest times.

So let's fly towards our death and watch us zoom right out of it.

OPTIMISM

I'm so in for it, I know it.
Something really great has to happen,
if I just live through this. I get so hopeless,
ashamed, doubtful and depressed
and I even think of suicide from time to time
but every painful tear that leaves my eyes
will be worth it.
There's got to be a light at the end of the tunnel
and I will keep walking in wonder.

I will feel the sun's rays as it bursts
from the black heavy clouds in my mind,
and I will find the rainbow after the storm.
I will find and I will climb out of this rock bottom hell,
rather than lay my cold bones to rest in it.
My life has hardly begun but it will soon and when it does,
I will find all of my problems,
I will climb my way out of them,
and I will fight for the will to live.

I have discovered my optimism.
I am stronger than this.

JUST FORGET ME, IT'S THAT EASY

Don't give up. Don't lose hope.

Please don't play me like a fucking joke.

Don't stop now. Don't let me down.

I only want to know what real love is like

through your beaming eyes,

but don't waste my time

because I can be without you just fine.

So don't fuck with my life.

You hardly know me

and nothing you're getting into.

I just want to see

if you know how to think things through.

I'm not asking you to be willing

to give your life to me.

I'm just wanting to think I'm worth saving,

and needing to feel I'm worth anything...

or will I just eternally

cause everyone to worry

over my suicidal tendencies?

Fuck it all, fuck everything. Just forget me.

Aromantic/Asexuality

I see how some of my friends who are in relationships,
and I remember from past experiences,
how your whole day can turn to shit in a flash of a second
just from a single, simple sentence.

I get some guys who question my emotions
and ask how I'm a lesbian,
and damn I feel bad for you straight women
but most guys really do just think with their dick.

As if I need to fuck them
to decide whether I could love them.
Can somebody educate them for me
the difference between romance and sexuality?

Some people are so stereotypical,
but I've been starting to think logical.
Do you ever think there's an identity
where there involves no uncontrollable feelings?

Of course, there's always emotional stability,
but what about aromanticism? Asexuality?
Question yourself when you last felt emotion
towards the opposite or same sex.

To be victimless from lust,
and free from the butterflies within
that eat up your insides
and leave you feeling dead and dry.

Not every couple chooses to have sex.
Not every marriage has love in it.
You don't have to answer anyone's questions
because your love and sex life is only your business.

Maybe one day, you're one way
then something else the next.
Who cares what they have to say,
as long as you're impressed.

Being in control of your emotions,
I'd never be able to possess a notion of,
and abstaining from sex,
I'd imagine would create the best love.

A Try

Do you think she could really care as more than a friend?
I think this is all in my head.
She leans against me so much and what about the touching?
I'm so lonely, I think my mind is making up stories.
I just need to know what you think.

It's not too often that I start feeling this way.
Could we just hang out alone today?
I've been so alone for so long and what's been going on?
I just want someone to wrap my arms upon.
How do you feel about this song?

Don't look to me now if I'm just a rebound.
You're going to have to show some effort for longer than this
if you are somehow someone who will stick around,
but there's no way I could ever deserve such happiness.

Please tell me my optimism is true this time.
I'm sick in my stomach of all the letdowns and lies
and you've always been there, so I think it's fair
we give it a try.

MISERY LOVES COMPANY

You say there are some things
we think we need but really don't,
but I swear I have to have this
or my sanity will be lost.
Broken, scarred and bleeding for life
with my mentality to sleep to at night.
Will there ever be anyone that understands
and let me know I'll be alright?
I'm snapping apart rubber bands
trying to get out of my mind.
The wider the length,
the farther it'll shoot
but I'm giving too much strength
trying to get through.
Why can't anyone else see the way I do?

We'll never know how things could have been
because I fucked up everything
and I'll never live this down on myself
but please don't feel bad for my hopeless soul.
There wasn't much you could have done.
Misery is just all I will know.

Every time I open my mouth,

something stupid comes out.

I wish to never speak again now,

shut myself down.

Perfection is so confusing,

we all want this, but it doesn't exist.

I always knew love can leave you blind

but alone can do it too sometimes

because it's all in the fear or in the bliss.

Now I realize I'll never complete my purpose

to find real and true happiness.

In the hardest way, I finally discovered today

perfection doesn't exist.

and no one can stop me from thinking and feeling like this.

Acceptance is my target, but I'll always miss.

AngeLove

It was a strange night when you came into my life
and we talked until four.
You say these sweet things that get me to think
you're not like others before.

Our feelings are forming so fast.
We're both so open – it's never been like that.
Could this love be the one that lasts?
You're really the sweetest thing I never had.
You're exactly the person I need.
You make me happy when I'm sad.
Please be the one who never leaves,
because I've already let my guard down for you.

I've just been dying lately for love to be true.
Promise you'll stay and never let the fire in our hearts fade,
maybe our love could last forever like the sun's flames.
Happily ever after like a fairytale,
where fantasies come real.

Let's make believe I was always the girl of your dreams.
Am I worth it enough, to get you to fall in love?
Could you change my world with your sweet words?
Looking into someone's eyes has never made me feel this alive
and when you're on my mind, I just get weaker inside.

I know it's late for Valentine's
but sweetness, will you be mine?

EUPHORIA

I don't know where you came from
but I'm melting like mud in the sun.
You know, the way it cracks and dries up?
You've opened my trust,
changing the world I know of...

You beamed from behind a cloud,
your brightness doesn't cease to astound,
turning my life around.
Heaven is where I'm bound
because I've got your love now.

As long as I'm near your smile and your eyes,
for a while in this life, I can feel alive.
Hearing your voice makes my problems subside.
I'm trying to find the words to write
to explain what I'm feeling inside.

Because it's so crazy but it's amazing,
the sensation I'm craving,
this feeling is lifesaving.
So don't leave me, I'm begging.
I don't want to forget this.

I want it forever.

I never want to get over,

I just want to feel closer

because I feel myself falling deeper,

promise you'll stay here with me still...

THANKS ASSHOLE

I know you like older girls
but a day away is not enough for your taste.
Now I have a girl older than yours
and any feeling I once knew for you is erased.

In the beginning, we all knew it'd end this way,
you were so out of focus, but I never gave up.
All you loved were drugs, and to think I could be one.
I've come to my senses and all you could say was sorry.

There's no way to mend this, all the shame and misery.
You are a big reason I am the person I am today.
The drugs and the distance pushed us away
and the changing of the seasons made it all okay.

The girl that told me never to forget her
has forgotten me
and I'll never again ever
be heartbroken in misery.

Good riddance bitch,
I hope you get all your wishes.
I've dug my ditches
and your memory is swimming with the fishes.

I've never met you, but I'll never forgive you.

You told me you loved me,

you told me I saved your life.

You told me we were destiny,

so I thought you could save mine,

but how could you when everything was just a lie?

You're nothing but a fucking secret in the back of my mind.

I know you couldn't miss me at all,

you're so much happier, my feelings for you are gone

and I am so lost.

I am so lost

and so gone.

Desperate Trysts and Ignorant Bliss

I know I'm confusing you.
I hope I'm not losing you.
My whole life feels hopeless,
but you give me hope.
I'm so damn used to being alone
and I'm just really, really scared.
I just want to hear that promise
that no matter what, you'll always be there
and through it all, you'll never stop caring.

I am staring down an inner ache.
I need to break this distance,
I need to feel your fingertips.
I want you to take me away,
you and me forever
cause I swear when we're together,
the whole world stands still.
It's incredible.

How is it possible
I've found an actual angel?
Please don't ever let go.
You're not even here
but I feel you getting close,
as if you were near.

I feel you from within
and I'm weakening.
This distance stings.

The days don't even phase me.
I'm just waiting till we can be.
I'm just counting down to the moment when
I can be with you and your eyes again.
I need the strength I receive from your eyes.
Please promise you'll never let this end,
I swear if I fall in love again,
I won't be coming out of this alive.

JUST A POEM YOU WON'T CARE TO KNOW

She is so scared to lose me

but in reality, if anything, I'm losing her.

How can I let this girl be my world?

She's so perfect but I'm so burnt.

I'm so apathetic.

This is the first time in weeks since I've written shit.

She loves me so much

and for the first time in years, I feel trust.

Am I really good enough?

She doesn't understand.

She doesn't get she's got to dig in deep,

like this one girl did,

sucked me inside like a monster sized leach

and now I'm going to do things to her

that the bitch did to me and all I can say is sorry

because I'm a piece of shit

that doesn't know how to fix anything

and even if I really am the one,

that doesn't mean she'll never want to leave.

All I ever wanted was true love,

the kind that will be real no matter what.

I was begging for her to come,

I really almost lost hope and gave up

and now in these next few months,

she's asking for too much.

I just want to have fun

but I don't want to lose her love

and I'm so fucking indifferent.

All I want to do is smoke, party and drink.

How can I get closer to her with this distance?

I'm so ignorant

and I know she can't stand it.

I'm independent with my emotions

and I don't like to let anyone in.

I'm desperate for anything

to break me within,

and I think she has the key

for me to let go of everything.

I'm so uninspired, I have no muse.

Smoking's getting old and drinking is an abuse.

I just want to feel something good for once,

please make me fall in love.

Just open me up and don't give up.

Never say what you think I want to hear
because bullshit always puts me in tears.
Can we just be happy for the rest of our years?
I'm a dumb bitch but I don't mean to make you scared.
Maybe I'm just too inexperienced to know what I feel.
All I know is I love you and I need you here.

YOUR TRUE LOVE IS A DRUNK IN THE CLUB

You're not the same it seems,

not the way you used to be

or at least not to me.

You feel so distant.

Have you lost interest?

What can I do to fix this?

What have I done to lose your heart?

I have to re-find my way back to your arms

or one more time,

one more bad fight,

and I'll forget all we had

but I don't want you as a passing fad.

You once said what we have is special

and it's only growing stronger.

I hope you know how you feel

or I won't stay much longer...

She leaves me to walk home alone and scared,

all I wanted was someone who cares.

At least give me a call
just to say goodnight
and that you'll always love me
for the rest of our lives.
I can't remember to forget her,
she's always on my mind.

You know the words you say,
well, in my head they stay
just to constantly re-play.
I guess I overanalyze,
I just want to understand how it works inside
your plotting mind.

Because now I'm scared and unsure,
you've made me insecure.
Now if you think I care, I don't.
If you think I'd miss you, I won't.
I've had it with this bullshit,
you're taking me for granted.

You don't know how much the words you say hurt.

You can't see how I'm so insecure.

You don't have a care in the world.

I'm just another stupid girl.

You have the nerve to ask, "why bother to try?"

You swore to me I was the love of your life,

but now I realize it was all a lie

and I think I'm just going to die so bye.

The Writing's On The Wall And Now I See It All

I used to be left shaking
when you pulled your fingers out of me,
crazy how just a touch
made me breathe so heavy.

You swore to me I was the love of your life,
I thought I found my reason for being alive.
Everything made sense and all was right.
Now you couldn't have a care of what happens to me.

I'm left wondering what is wrong with me?
It's nothing I can see.
Can I be fixed, or should I turn to the dirt?
I swear I can't stand another day in this world.

She never really ever cared for me.
I knew I could never be the love of your life.
Always and forever is a lie because everybody dies
and I can't even cry because I'm just so numb inside.

Everything and everybody is fucking up.
Nothing feels right, like heaven left the sky.
There is no such thing as real love,
just lies, deceit and a shame full of lust.

Nobody will ever grow up.
I'm sorry, I've heard it enough.
How could it be real
when there's no such thing as real love?

Forever is what I want.
Love, no matter what.
Who won't always jump
to just breaking up.

I gave away too much yet again,
just to get thrown away, left in bitter regret.
How long would it take my friends to forget?
It's too late for me to try to make things perfect.

No one wants to help me, I'm just a stupid fuck up
and I'm way too easy to fuck with.
I'm so fucking worthless.
Everybody just forget me.

CORRUPTION

I don't want you for the weekend.
I don't want you for the summer.
I want you forever.
Please don't leave
because I need
something to believe in.

My life is slipping.
It's like as if I'm always hitting rock bottom
and there's just no stopping.
Shit just got fucked.
I'm in a holding cell with handcuffs.
Still drunk but the hangover is coming up.

The girl with her head down
and hair over her face,
she needs to get out of this town,
away from this place, away from the pain.
She's losing sanity and security.
Corrupted friends steal away her purity.

Give me that fork
and let me stick it in the outlet.
I'd rather not live anymore
with this bullshit.

She's just a liar,
that's all I see in her.

You're just a fucking liar.
You don't need to worry for me.
What are you, crazy?
We were never meant to even speak.
Hate me or forget me,
just stop fucking texting me.

Big part of your life my ass,
that's why you'll leave it all in the past.
You made your choice so fuck off.
It's okay for you to be human but I won't be soft
because it wasn't okay for me
but you never understood anything.
In a few years, you'll be long forgotten.
Remember, you made the decision.

Love is a deadly germ,
corrupting hopeless Earth.
Contained in simple words people say,
in between all the looks your ex gave.
An emotion thriller, a thought killer,
A soul drainer, a vision strainer.

Sometimes I like to pretend she's around looking for me,
and she's full of regret and that she's sorry
but it's all bullshit, I know,
because she forgot me long ago.
I really need to accept what's done is done
and what's gone is gone
and I have to let it all go if I want to move on.

Everything will be fine.
Things will work out in time.
Yeah we all die,
but there's so much more to life
than the infinity beyond outer space.
There's got to be more than our rotting grave.

TOP OF THE WORLD

It's like I've died.
My emotions have dried after drowning in my cries
but you are my sunshine.
You restore my life and now I'm alive.

I can't say this enough
that I desperately need your love.
I'd drop to my knees and kiss your feet,
all you have to say is please.
You are everything I need.

I will never give up, no matter what.
I will never stop, no matter the cost.
I hope to put you on top of the world
because it's all an angel like you deserves.

This isn't even the beginning,
wait until I'm living with you
and all our wishes and dreams will come true.
A kiss is all it will take to dissipate away the pain
and into those eyes I'll fall. I want to give you my all.

ANGEL ON EARTH

You can always make me smile.
You're someone I really admire
and someone I really, truly cherish.
It's so magical when we kiss.

I adore you so much,
always craving for your touch.
You inspire me again.
For that, I have a lot of respect.

In fact, I've never felt so blessed.
Your love keeps me in check.
You know I care beyond words.
You are my angel on Earth.

09/08/2008

THE LOVE I HAVE BEEN MISSING

It's too much, all at once
but at the same time, just enough.
You melt my stone, black heart into a puddle
just thinking of the ways we cuddle.
I wish I was with you too
but we'll be together soon enough sweetness.
Just got to have some faith and patience,
I know I do.

You're who I really want to stick with.
I honestly never thought I'd get to feel like this.
I've never felt so secure or sure about anybody before.
You know I'm all yours.
I'm trying too,
to get a car and see you more.
I'm trying and it's all I can do
but I won't give up, I will pursue.

I wish I was there or anywhere.
I just wish I was with you,
to play fight over who is more silly.
I'd shush you up and give you a kissy
while holding you so close to me.
I want to cuddle too,
and stare into those eyes and tell you I love you.
Oh, the things we'd do.

I love you and I need you.

Do you know you mean everything to me?

I don't believe you have a clue.

You are so amazing.

Incredible beyond explanation.

No, it is explainable,

because you are an angel.

I can hardly wait,

just to show you I feel the same.

Yes I do, don't argue.

You make my heart melt and my body so weak.

You have the power to do whatever you'd want to me.

It's crazy to trust but for you, I am crazy.

You make it so easy to believe, you're my everything.

I finally found the love I have been missing.

WHAT'S THE WORTH OF WORDS
WHEN THE ACTION HOLDS THE PASSION

I'm still sorry that I hurt you and made you cry.

I wish I could hold you and say sorry a million times.

I wish I knew how to describe this feeling,

it's like everywhere and everything.

I'm out of my mind, going crazy inside.

I love you too much to even contain.

I love you so much to ever explain.

You make love just a 4-letter dictionary word.

The feelings overcoming me are out of this world.

I'm sorry I don't know how to be,

just waiting for you to finally

give up on me.

Be like everybody, but you just won't be.

You know exactly what to say to open my eyes.

My whole heart is beating with your life.

You've brought out the best in my mind

and helped me realize

there's this goal I will never let go.

So Crazy

My heart is burning in hell.
A million sharp pins are stabbing my brain.
I know I cannot be well,
this feeling cannot be sane.
You just don't understand,
how weak I really am.
You don't get it,
I'm truly pathetic.

Please make me not so crazy,
tell me everything's okay.
My insecurities are taking over me
and I can't believe you are feeling the same way.

You must be totally honest
because I'm way too obsessive.
I overanalyze every sentence
and it all makes me so sensitive.
Now I'm so helpless like I'm dying
because I'm worthless even after trying.
Nothing is okay, we can't talk.
I'm left scared with these negative thoughts.

MY STRENGTH IS IN YOUR FAITH

You're such an angel,

is it wrong for me to think you deserve better?

I want to give you the moon and stars,

as cliché as that sounds.

You just don't know how perfect you are.

You complete my empty heart.

Please understand. Please care.

The only two things I ask.

I'm sorry I just get a little scared.

My mind sometimes gets attacked.

I'm such a nuisance.

Is it okay to feel so ridiculous like this?

I'm sorry you found me an annoying mess,

at least I wasn't over the edge.

Although you have the power to turn me around.

The love I feel for you is too strong for bounds.

Just tell me everything is okay
so my world can keep on turning.
Remind me you'll love me every day
so my stomach can stop churning.

TO MY SENSES, TO MY KNEES

Love can be so much to take in

but when you know it's real, it's worth everything.

I want to get lost in your eyes.

I want to embrace you all the time.

I feel more like myself when you call me baby.

You know that feeling? That sense of security.

I can't explain it, but you are home to me.

Honestly, I've never been so positive about anybody.

I can't wait to get you close to me.

I'll pull you in closer than you ever thought you could be.

I love you so much.

I can't say it enough.

Cuddling will be our profession.

You bring out my passive-aggression,

because you got me restless

when we are disconnected.

You bring me to my senses,

you bring me to my knees.

I know why things never worked with my exes,

I understand why things could never be.

Everything I learned from them,

everything that happened back then,

and I take it to this,

and this is it.

I know now, I'll settle down.

I believe in this love. I trust in you.

I know things will fall in place for us, they have to.

EGO OVERFLOW

I'm sorry, although I never was good enough.

Everything I ever said was everything I ever meant

and too much you've never heard enough of,

and everything I've never felt before.

I couldn't bear to put this on hold.

Every day I expected more,

but every day was the same old

and I never believed it could happen,

I never thought I could feel myself slippin'.

Everything between us was magic.

I never doubted you for a minute

but here it is, you starting over again,

me loathing my reflection.

We never even had a chance.

Don't act like we do when we don't.

Your past acquaintances were insane but don't blame the herb.

TV radiation kills the same, if not more brain cells, than to smoke.

At least I know how to research.

It seems your pride is too sure.

I remember in the beginning

how you finished my sentences

but every time I felt more butterflies,

I was always under the influence.

It's depressing, I'm so ridiculous.

You can't save everyone, I guess.

Now you see I'm hopeless.

Go ahead and believe I'm a liar.

I and all your exes are way too similar.

Now I wonder how being friends will really work out.

I don't think I can live with myself with what I've lost now.

I have so many flaws I don't know how to fix.

I'm equivalent to a wall when it comes to dealing with shit

and we're not going to work when you can't understand it.

Don't act like you do when you don't.

Your past acquaintances were insane but don't blame the herb.

TV radiation kills the same, if not more brain cells, than to smoke.

At least I know how to research.

It seems your pride is too sure.

Ruined Human

Can you be more descriptive and literate?

Why sleep on that side and I sleep on this?

I sit here, just can't stop thinking.

It's been so long since I felt this feeling.

My musing is trying to make sense of some things.

I never get what I give in return.

I never get what I fucking deserve.

Why is it so complicated

for you to recognize that I need appreciation?

Anything to help me just know

I am worth the energy, time and space.

Am I of any value to you?

Are you thankful for anything I do?

We are not on the same page.

Slam my doors and I'll run away.

I'll find a way to escape,

not to be controlled and told how to breathe each breath.

I'm not the smartest but I know those aren't the right steps.

Do you recognize all these hints of neediness for you?
Walk away and leave if you can't confront the truth
I am abandoned in my solitude
in the wrath of my own mind.
Maybe I deserve the restrictions of these confines
but no, it's not right. That's not life.

Why can't I just be loved or cared for?
Respected. Appreciated.
I don't feel in the least bit precious or pure.
In fact, I feel my soul is totally wasted.
Am I human? I am ruined.

Why can't you recognize my acknowledgment?
Can you be more descriptive and literate?
Please prove to me I'm dating a person of intellect.
I find it difficult to commit in this relationship.
I see you in the fucking scum of nicotine spit.
I hate you're so lazy and taken name over my shit.

Am I human? I am ruined.
My purity concurs to be.
I can't fall in love
when my standards don't match up.
I wonder if they'll ever see.

Energy, Time, Space

She doesn't want me anymore.

She doesn't care about anything that happens.

She doesn't want to stay here.

You fucking suck.

That's all there is.

Everything turns into a secret.

Life is pitiful.

Don't sleep. There's no time.

It's being lost every moment.

I sit here and stare,

how much longer till you care?

I envision you there

miserably ever after,

suffering in your nightmare.

Burning every single fairy tale.

Your life is my jail.

I can see this spiraling black circle consuming you

and flushing you away.

How could you have nothing to apologize for?

And make it seem like it's all my fault?

2You were wrong.

I know I failed

but I admit to my shames.

You over there,
you're such a fucking disgrace.

You stole the poems I wrote to you.
You've probably burned those too.
The way you burned everything I love about life.
You're no savior or Jesus Christ.
The only way I could be saved,
energy, time and space.
My saving grace.

01/26/2008

Purpose For The Pain

I wish she would come back.
Is there anybody else that could be like that?
I doubt it hurt so bad.
Focusing on forgetting the past like an ass.

I want to isolate, not get attached.
I am all I will ever have.
Until I disintegrate,
I will not reciprocate.

I can only stay positive for so long
until my own mentality gives out on me.
I'll just lay all alone with the lights off,
contemplating, judging and spacing.

Letting my thoughts absorb,
going somewhere to hide from the world
and not co-exist with this reality anymore.
It could always be worse.

There's love and hate all over the place.
Angels and demons in every thought and emotion.
It's all so crazy to process some days,
on others, it's a little easier to be human.

I don't know how my life's going to work out.

I don't want to get my hopes up for anything now.

I don't know which direction to go from here.

I can only act on how I feel.

I hope you see the reasons of my actions

is because I can't see any of it as lasting,

in a bigger picture worth grasping,

in a promise for a meaning,

living more than breathing.

PATH OF REDEMPTION

I wonder if I'll ever feel again
like there's someone that just gets me.
I want to be a positive impact.
I want to find healing consciously constantly.
I wonder how you controlling your memory has worked out,
how you took advantage of my psychic abilities.
Your whole existence has shaped me, now changed me
and I still can't believe it's all over that quickly.
The scold you told to me
has bestowed a control on me to become holy.
You have no idea how surreal you made me feel.
You couldn't ever hear, you just wanted to repeal.
You were stuck on your ex and now I'm so depressed,
I told you to forget me and finally you listened.
You called me crazy and angry
and I couldn't feel the difference of light.
Everything was without life.

Now I'm on a path of redemption.
I am enlightened by my new vision.
A fresher perspective of new beginnings.
An incentive on true gold winnings.

Passive Flare

When your breathing is synchronized with mine,

there is no time,

only thoughts and feelings so divine

as we are intertwined.

I want to rub your thighs

and get inside.

I'll show you everything with my eyes.

I know I'm not the most intelligent

but having you here has shown me so blessed.

When you commence to undress

I'm so lucky to have you to depend on.

Without any makeup

your cheeks become

such a cute pink.

Your lips, a moisturized red

and upon your chest, the promise ring

hanging around your neck.

You're always so stunning

but I'm like a pen running out of ink.

I wish I could describe your skin,

how beautiful and soft it is,

so gorgeous, so let me gorge right in.

Can I just lay here?

I think I have a fever.

Nothing seems clear

except that I miss her.

I know you didn't ask,

I'm sorry for expressing.

I know the way I'm acting

is slightly more obsessive... depressing.

I feel like I'm spinning, maybe I'm concussed.

Okay I'll admit, I'm definitely in lust.

Should I stop thinking too much

or am I even thinking enough?

I'm writing you this poem

only to let you know

I swear I love you more

than I am capable to show.

Your sexual innuendos

has me so devout to you.

You've inspired me again.
You keep me lifted.
You're my best friend.
You have my soul within.

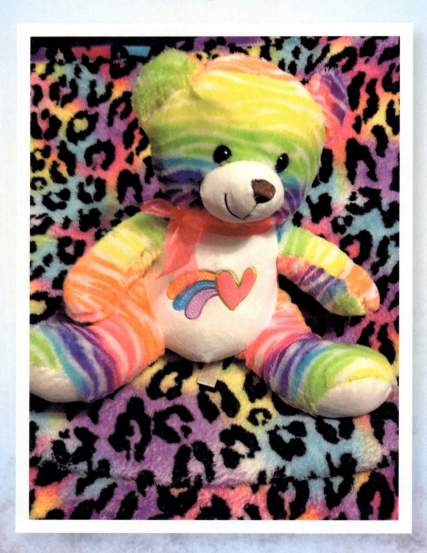

Charades & Antics

It's time to place my bets.
Don't forget your 'best friend'
(I meant me; it must be tough sorting through them.)
The one who paid for you and your ex-girlfriend's rent
twice and more than a million times you take me for granted.

It's been such a long time coming…
so it's going to take more for me to be courageous
to just ignore your fucking texts.
I'm done with how fucking weak I get,
how weak I am, to deserve this in the end?

I GET IT. I'm not important.
Look at all your magnificent,
expensive, valuable new clothes and shoes.
I hope a fire turns to ash all that's in your shit hole of a bedroom,
including the friendship book I bought for you.

I'll never again ever let anyone fuck me over as bad as you have
and I truly believe no one else will ever come close.
No one has nearly been as shitty to me as you though.
So congrats on sucking hardcore fucking ass
but I'm the bigger dumbass, we know that.

I tried to be hate-free but it only made me feel angry.

I just want to write good poetry, but everything seems corny.

Just stick to what you have in front of you.

Fucking forget me.

The way it's meant to be.

INK FROM THE PEN
CAN'T KEEP UP WITH THOUGHTS IN MY HEAD

Sometimes it's better to forget

than ever make amends.

I really do wonder

how I could have ever

felt a connection to her.

Why almost a decade later,

she can feel like such a stranger

but so much greater.

It clouds my mind

as I wait for the bugs to eat me alive.

She kills me as I drown in her thoughts.

She's so calm, sincere and composed.

I'm the absolute opposed.

It seemed like heaven beamed

right through my window

when I saw the 10 familiar digits,

it was really only my happiness

but I thought it was purpose.

It clouds my mind
as I wait for the bugs to eat me alive.

I'm Crazy Eyes
in her Alex and Piper life
as I try to figure out what it is about
texts from her that create this world.
Constructed together
for the viewing pleasure.
I wish I could stop thinking about her.
It would make everything better.

The months go by,
will I forget the first love of my life?
It clouds my mind
as I wait for the bugs to eat me alive.

BUY BULL

The bible is so intense,
so much of it doesn't make sense.
Father, Son, Holy Spirit.
Please give me your blessings.
I don't trust anybody.
What is right? What is wrong?
I don't believe anyone.

Where is my mom?
Was she filled with evil?
Is that why she was diseased with cancer?
God I feel terrible.
My only way for an answer
is through prayer.

Right now, I am scared.
All my life, I felt this fear
of rejection... is it all real?
Am I damned to hell for the way I feel?
None of this matters to any of them
but I used to cut myself over this.

"You're going to hell."
I remember when they used to tell me it
because I was gay and dressed "gothic"
and it made me into a more worse person
than I should've been, but I was just a kid.

I can see myself burning…
I know I'm not perfect…
for so long I felt worthless.
Am I a work of the devil?
Am I just mentally unstable??
NOTHING MAKES SENSE.
THAT'S what's worthless.

BAD LUCK

One way to beat writer's block
is to just keep writing
but what is there to write about
that's actually exciting?
Get my thoughts out,
a brigade of how?
Brainstorming, heartwarming.
Past forming, rest assuring.

Every night at my job, I clean
to get out.
Every night is the same routine,
I black out.
I need new glasses
but with pizza as my passion,
money, I am lacking.
Eventually I'll make it happen.
There's just so much distraction.

I have a rip on my lip.
My girlfriend says it's because I don't use chap stick
but I think it's because I'm cursed with
all this madness, this bad luck.
Every little thing adds up.
Was that sound of the wind or a car engine?

Is the furnace making music?
I'm starting to lose it.

Lately I've been feeling like shit.
I'm seeing a lot of the number six
and I'm getting caught on the wrong side of things.
I think my ghosts are evil.
Where are the angels?
Bad luck still resumes
every which way I move.
My regrets don't understand.
Follow me, not again.

I remember the way we used to talk.
Years later, morbid fucking thoughts.
God, I need your guidance at all times.
I'm lost and stranded without direction.
I need a sign; I need a message.
Repentance, acceptance, redemption, progression.
I know these are the steps.
I need to access it with my perspective.

Scratching at the skin on my head
like I'm trying to open the door to the basement
or pull down the ladder going up to the attic.
As I twist and rip, trying to pry within,
trying to figure out something,
the blood pours again, it hurts to touch it.
This will never mend; I will never begin.
An answer to my questions is all I wanted
but I have to be the one to resolve this.

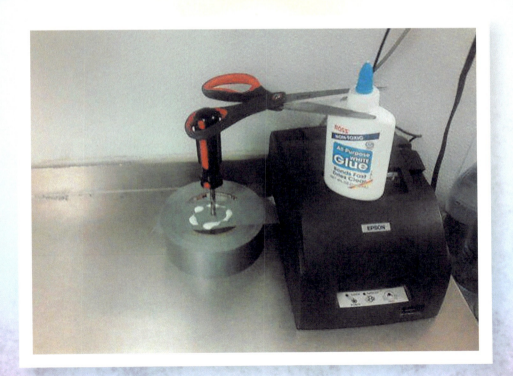

Counterculture

I feel like puking
because I want to know what you're doing
or how you can be so happy,
the way you do that so magically.
Maybe it's all just a dream, a nightmare, an idea
like the way I feel could ever be real.
I blame my writer's block on how we don't talk.
Every time she fucks up – I miss you, it's screwed.
Here I am.. longing for you.
I can't forget … if it's all true.
I'll always look past
the flaws that push it back.

I could start tally marking the years on the walls,
like they do in prison,
to keep track of time before they're free.
I could take lots of pills to keep calm,
to stop the thinking,
to help me go straight to sleep.
Maybe somehow
in a world I will never know about,
everything won't fucking revolve around you.
Maybe somehow
in a life I'm struggling to see,
you'll only be a forgotten memory.

I'm laughing over a situation that will never happen
and it's tragic.
I'm waiting every second for you to send me a message,
it's pathetic.
I'm yearning and searching for the slightest evidence
that you might give a shit
but it's pointless
and I should forget this.

I'm too dependent on you.
The words you say mean so much more than others do.
You're not just some imaginary idea.
Once upon a time, you were real.
Now your face is missed less
the longer your absence.

GOOD RIDDANCE TO BAD RUBBISH

I'll have you know I'm getting over you.

Slowly but surely, it's the truth

and maybe one day, you won't be my muse.

I know someday is so long overdue.

You never cared, everything was always for your benefit.

Now it's time I exist for my own cause.

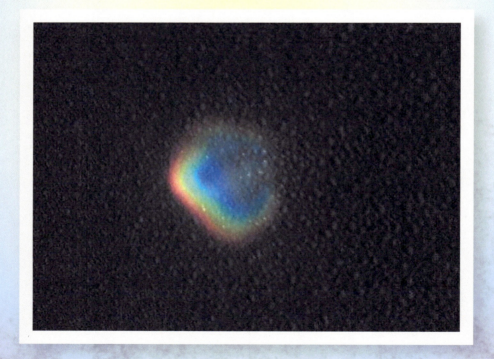

I'll see to it – the power of your words will have an end to it.

I just hope I can find the strength to move on.

I'll leave you right where you belong, in the fucking past.
Our reality wasn't built to last.
It never was real at all.
Tell me, was it wrong to try to construct
an honest friendship that only destructs..
but I could never break your walls.

How many months or years will go by this time?
Will you never again say hi? That you're doing fine?
I know you still read my blog
judging and feeding off every sob
and that's cool, you know I trusted you
but every day, I'm mogging away..
Your existence will be gone from my brain
because you're the one that blocked me in the first place.

THE AMERICAN DREAM VERSUS PERSONAL PROGRESS

I really hate being awake during the day.
The only time I appreciate the sunshine
is when it's 90 degrees and I'm at the beach.

I love the summer
and I love the spring
but it's the middle of winter.

This isn't supposed to be happening.
I really don't like global warming,
when nature is unnatural, what a disaster.

People say that other people
aren't supposed to be homosexual,
your old age accusations granted from the bible.

It won't make you any better,
won't make you any wiser.
A righteous higher power wouldn't accept judgmental liars.

The world is spinning, people are sinning.
There is no winning for what they're spindling.
Their miserable ending.

Holy shit, what an epiphany.
Life is catastrophically
changing everybody.

HATRED IS A WASTE OF TIME, KEEP AN OPEN MIND

I fucking love my life. Everything I have is enough to suffice.

The new snow causes a brighter glow of the night,

the night is pure.

A girl in my left arm and a cat in my right,

late Monday night or early Tuesday morning,

you are snoring until the sun's glow through the window

on the table past the blanket where the rainbow cup sits.

The alcoholic drink is finished but I haven't yet put it in the sink.

I had too much to think, I got stuck, I never got up.

My religion is smoking weed and finding inner peace.

Keeping an open mind, and be kind to everyone,

all the while loving life.

The sun on the world right now looks like a painting,

radiating.

I can't believe we're alive in it,

breath taking.

I'll never get anywhere with sleeping all the time.

I'm going to make this day, make this life mine.

THE WEAK WILL DIE, THE STRONG SURVIVE

"Why do they only bite you and not me?"

You said as I pointed to the bug on the wall.

You were really tired but it seemed

you only cared if it affected you at all.

Why didn't she kiss me goodnight?

Why did she close her eyes

before making sure everything was alright?

I need to disappear far away from here.

I'm not afraid, one day you'll wake

and I'll already be gone away.

Don't think I'll stay,

there's nothing left here for me anyway.

I've got what I came here for,

now I'm ready to explore.

You can't tie me down, I'm bored.

I deserve so much more.

I'm really over everyone's sarcastic humor.

Nothing's funny about how fucked up everything is.

I look forward to be in a drunken stupor

trying to forget about all that's negative.

You don't like sad music but you love shows involving death.

Watching Netflix for hours on end will sure help you forget

the life you're living, it isn't what you wanted.

Like some big suspense plot, but during it, the show's stopped.

You're not afraid, one day I'll wake
and you'll already be gone away.
Don't think you'll stay,
there's nothing left here for you anyway.
You've got what you came here for,
now you're ready to explore.
I can't tie you down, you're bored.
You deserve so much more.

You say I'm so harshly critical,
but honestly, at least I tell the truth.
I'm sorry I have grown so bitter
but I'm not for being honest with you.
Stress is a strain that never goes away
when your home is more than you can afford.
Your shitty friends thought it would be okay
to take advantage then walk out the door.
I guess you should never depend upon anyone.
Life is a bitch and the truth hurts.
I wonder about God when I'm at rock bottom.
I wonder if karma will do the works.

I wish my mom was still around,
going on seven years without her face or voice.
There's a heaviness in my throat now.
Nothing was ever a fucking choice.

SLEEPING ON THE LEFT

Life will never get easier.
The only person I wanted was her.
Nothing will ever get better.
I need everything to fade into blurs.

I watched a firetruck from the rearview head towards Maple Oaks
and I wonder about our hellhole.
Maybe the place would just set ablaze
but I'll never forget feeling so alone.

I hope your heart drops like the way mine did,
when you pushed me off the fucking cliff.
You can't blame me for this devastation
with no thoughts except inebriation and self-mutilation.

Don't say you never lied.
You told me many times you were in love & wanted to marry me.
Don't say you never stole and destroyed what was mine,
being with you has more than fucked with my mentality.

Just because you do things no one else can see
doesn't mean you can get away so easily.
Your naivety is something embedded in you, just like my attitude
which I gained from struggling to survive what I've been through

Fuck you for blaming me
for your insecurities.
Please, never again speak
unless it's an apology.

If I Write Something, It's Better Than Nothing

As you age, the faster life goes.

In that case, I never want to get old.

Even though the concept of life and death is really scary,

I feel very lucky we are alive simultaneously.

There's a lot of things I can be grateful for.

I don't have any mental or physical disorders.

I'm perfectly normal.

The pit on my patio is too small for the fires I aspire for,

kind of like my mind, without rhymes.

I'm dying for something of lore, something more.

I need to be more logical with my feelings,

I've been getting too emotional over anything/everything.

I'm so jaded and my desires are faded.

I don't think I satisfy her sexually or romantically.

The only thing I know how to do is give her my money,

that always makes people happy.

I don't think that maybe she ever thought I was more than cute,

let alone beautiful, or even pretty.

I'm fucking rude, even from my dreams, I wake up angry.

Am I just withdrawing? I'll probably let it kill me.

But I just want to heal. It's so hard to feel.

It's hard when you do and it's hard to do...

I'll probably just die here.
I wish I could heal. I just want to feel.
It's hard to do and then it's hard when you do...
Please don't let me just die here.

Falling Down At Your Front Door

All we do is drive
wishing we had the strive
to improve our lives.
Getting away from the gray clouds
of Middletown
because Columbus
has more fun in store for us.
I'm doing what I know is best,
keeping this sealed in my chest.
This doesn't have to progress.

I don't want to go inside.
I want to see you arrive
and to know you're alright.
We could fight through this life
together and never be alone.
Everyone wants to run away.
I can't even handle
the way I feel sometimes.
Why can't anybody just stay?
I need to settle and find a home.

Why should I care what you're doing?
You use me like everybody.
Maybe I'm just stupid..
It's just a silly dream
to think there's something in between.
Please don't take this personal.
I just miss someone to kiss
and have sex with.
There's no way I should have my feelings involved.
Everything eventually dissolves.

THERE IS BEAUTY IN YOUR BROKEN FORTITUDE

I'm tired of feeling numb
but you won't give me your love.
You're doing your thing, having' fun
but I wish you would be my one.
You say your head's a tornado,
a mess that you can't control.
Do you feel deep in your soul
it's time to let it all go?
What we have could be lasting.
So tell me if you have a hard time grasping
the idea of us is hard to imagine
but babe, I'm grabbing.

You deserve deliverance
from all the shit you've dealt with.
You deserve redemption
from all the chaos you've been in.
I'd give you my heart but it's broken.
I'd rather give you something worth holding.

A car flew down the street like a shooting star,
the moment I touched your arm
and I know it's not meant to be.
I know from deep inside me,
I just want to help you feel happy.

I wish I could do something as you sleep
so peacefully but I need to leave.
I'll anxiously write this note to let you know you're beautiful
even with all your scars and flaws,
your stories to tell.
I wish I could make you well
but I can't, you have to save yourself.

TRANSCENDENT PONDERER

The right things to say,

I'll never know how to control

what enters my brain.

Either too much or not enough.

Right now, it pours in waves.

Can you manipulate

the way I operate?

Teach me how to balance

crazy, raging emotions.

Label me toxic with problems

only I can solve if I acknowledge

and conquer them

but I think I'd rather

never hear from you again.

I believe I'm happier

without restrictions as your friend.

I should really know better.

I'm definitely not some puppet

You don't love me for who I am.

You don't care, you never did.

You just wanted me for sex

and you got it, everything you wanted

out of me and now I'm floating off the deep end.

Sitting on the bench by the pond.

The starry night sky engulfing our bodies.

I felt a romantic bond, with you sitting beside me

and besides you being on acid,

I really wish the moment could've lasted.

You were on another planet, blasted away from here.

I could've swore there was something more in our atmosphere

but the stars are not ours and you will disappear.

Nothing is real. Nothing is what it appears

After Riot Fest, in Chicago on the beach

past midnight, in the dark with the waves and the breeze.

I really wanted you to kiss me, Bre

but you stayed far away from me.

I know it's my fault I let you into my heart.

If only I could stop pretending

like I could be anything

at all to anyone.

I give up. Let this be done.

You don't love me for who I am.

You don't care, you never did.

You just wanted me for sex

and you got it, everything you wanted

out of me and now I'm floating off the deep end.

She's got me all figured out and now she's bored
and I want to end my life even though it's not bad
but it's the worst thing I've endured.
She's like a drug I need to give up
but I gave up so much for.
I'd rather be dead than to try anymore.
My writing keeps me alive, but my writing fucking sucks.
I'll never find the help I need. I just need hope
but it's nowhere to be seen, what a fucking joke.

Erase Everything

I can't be alone too long.

This pain is haunting

everything that has gone wrong.

My thoughts are taunting.

What happened to you?

You used to mean everything to me.

What happened to me?

I used to be the girl of your dreams.

We talked about getting married

and you're already engaged to somebody new.

How can you be so damn shady?

Forgetting everything and all we've ever been through.

I sit outside and breathe in the 4am air.. and a cigarette.

I feel so fucking ashamed of it all.

The truth is, I am the only one who will care... of all my regrets.

This loneliness will drown me without stall.

I'm pleading for a purpose.

What did I do to deserve this?

My life started sucking

when I let love in.

Unhealthy

All she will do is say hey,
make small conversation.
How does it fuck up my brain?
It gives me delusions.
Maybe I'm crazy
or lucky enough to know -
she was never a friend to me.
She was never anything, need the door closed.

I wish she could drop off the face of the earth
but I love writing for her.
I wish she would leave me the fuck alone.
The source of her power is unknown.
Maybe you should just forget my existence
and if you can't,
maybe you can explain why you couldn't
and understand.

Sometimes it seems like I could sleep forever
and it wouldn't even matter.
It wouldn't matter if I died
because I don't feel alive
unless you're talking to me.
How's that for unhealthy?

I was 13 when she took my heart

and it was 13 years on again, off again, being friends.

Truth is, she never wanted to give me a chance.

I wasn't what she wanted and I'll always wonder what if.

Sometimes I wish I had a different first love,

anyone who wouldn't have been so easy to imagine the world of.

It was the way she cared.

No one could ever compare, I swear.

I could sit out here all afternoon

as if you'd be here soon.

I'm stuck by myself in this realm.

All these years with the way I feel

and I wonder if I'll ever wind up

writing more about you in the future.

I've written about you longer

than I can remember.

She Drinks For The Taste, I Drink To Forget My Face

Nothing to say...
probably because she doesn't feel the same
but it's okay...
I need to know my place.

I wish I could do something
that would make you love me
but there's no connection with us,
never was and never will be.

I wish we could be like the beginning.
I wish I could keep you that happy
but it's all fleeting and temporary.
Now everything's so empty.

I wish I could be like you, so driven and strong.
You don't need anyone in the world
to tell you that you're wrong
or anyone at all.

The sun was rising
as we were driving.
Your head is in the clouds.
Nothing holds you down.

Who could keep you grounded?
Everyday I'm so astounded
at the way you think and carry yourself through.
You don't know but you've changed me with your point of view.

I wish I could somehow mean something to you
but to you, nothing lasts and you can't grasp me.
What would've happened if I could turn around
and turn my back on you?

I wonder if I'll ever feel amazement
again from someone who could be so amazing.
You're just a maze of a mind.
Fuck it, at least I actually tried.

I always sought validation from the approval of others
until you taught me the importance of loving myself the most.
My low self-esteem was toxic and held me from true happiness.
It's only ironic that you're my fulfilling dream trapped in nascence.

THE MUSIC

I don't really follow a lot of poets but I listen to a lot of music
and I own over a hundred CDs, I want to turn it into thousands.
I want to write words that have power to heal
like Mary Lambert or Nikita Gill.
My poetry is my history.
The CDs are the soundtrack melodies,
all my origin of inspiration.
Poetry is my salvation.

The stuff I wrote is what helped me cope,
Sad lyrics in music can help you gain emotional maturity.
Pain makes you wiser and stronger with refreshing clarity.
Some people go to church, I like to go to concerts.
The music is empowerment of something more
when I walk through those venue doors.
I love leaving the world behind
and all the bullshit lies I've grown to endure.

I had a dream somebody needed my help
and they actually cared about how I felt.
It's sad but it's true,
no one really gives a fuck about you
but it's even better when you come out a winner.

Never let go of any inner goals
and everyday little by little,
you might have something to show for.